Ute York

Living by the Moon

A Practical Guide for Choosing the Right Time

Ute York

Living by the Moon

A Practical Guide for Choosing the Right Time

Bluestar Communications®
Woodside, California

This book was originally written in German. In translating the text to English, the editors have attempted to find and include the original English language source for all quoted material.

Translated by Edith Zorn and Athene Bengtson, Goddess Enterprises
First published in German under the title
Mondzeit
Ein praktischer Ratgeber zur Nutzung der geheimnisvollen Kräfte des Mondes

44 Bear Glenn
Woodside, CA 94062
Tel: 800-6-Bluestar

Edited by Jude Berman
Cover Art by Garret Moore, Dreaming Lizard Studios

First printing 1997

ISBN: 1-885394-15-2

Library of Congress Cataloging-in-Publication Data

York, Ute.
[Mondzeit. English]
Living by the moon : a practical guide for choosing the right time / Ute York.
p.. cm.
Includes bibliographical references and index.
ISBN 1-885394-15-2
1. Astrology. 2. Moon--Miscellanea. 3. Moon--Influence on man.
I. Title.
BF1723.Y6713 1997
133.5--dc20 96-9337
CIP

Printed in USA

Contents

Part II

The Influence of the Moon on Health and Beauty

Part III

Your Personal Moon
Moon Rules for Family, Career and Everyday Life

Part IV

The Moon and Magic

Part V

The History of Moon Astrology

For my friends, the contadini of Sasso Pisano in Tuscany. Without them, I would never have known about the mysterious powers of the moon.

How Everything Began

It began, of course, at the full moon, on a warm summer night in Tuscany. We were sitting with friends having a glass of wine. The children were playing hide-and-go-seek in the bright moonlight. All of a sudden, ten-year-old Maggie came running to her mother, complaining that the warts on the soles of her feet hurt.

"Why don't *you* get rid of them?" my children asked me, as they looked up into the clear night sky. "We have a full moon."

Maggie was somewhat doubtful, but her parents and the other adults, who sat in the bower sipping their glasses of deep red Nero wine, were outright skeptical. They mocked such a childish superstition.

My daughter Jennie comforted her friend. "Don't be afraid. It'll work. Mama does it with us all the time."

Of course, it does work. I don't know why I'm able to charm warts. I only know that I can. However, the spell only succeeds when performed during a full moon.

I encouraged Maggie, "Look at the moon. It's able to move entire oceans. The tides appear because of its gravity. It's easy for it to get rid of these few warts."

Obligingly, Maggie looked up and nodded. We performed our little ritual. After one week, the warts fell off the soles of her feet—no problem.

The problem began later, however, when the children asked, "What else can the moon do besides taking away warts and making tides?"

I had to admit that I did not know. I started to ask friends, "Do you know anything about the mysterious forces of the moon?"

At first, none of our intelligent friends in Munich had any ideas beyond, "I had an uncle who was a lunatic," or "What about the menstruation cycle?"

Then, when I had almost given up, I found myself standing in the kitchen one day with my friend Neda. We were in the little village in Tuscany where we had summered for many years and I was in the middle of making jam. Neda is a farmer's wife and a gifted cook—the best, the women of Sasso, who are all good cooks, admit without jealousy. Without even looking into the exquisitely fragrant pot, Neda said, "I'm sorry, but that won't work."

"And why not?" I asked, insulted.

"Perché la luna non é buona," Neda answered with compassion. "Because, the moon's position isn't right. You can't cook jam while the moon is waxing."

I only could shake my head. Sure enough, two months later, my wonderful apricot jam was moldy. Then it occurred to me that I had been asking the wrong people; if I wanted to know about the mysterious powers of the moon, I had to seek elsewhere.

The first source was our Tuscan village; in other words, peasant wisdom. I learned from Giovanni, who brings our firewood, that a tree can only be felled at certain times if it is going to burn properly. I discovered that Fiorienza, who knows everything about animals, puts eggs under her brooding hens during the waxing moon so that healthier, stronger chicks will hatch. My neighbor Gastone revealed that my cucumbers, tomatoes, onions, and potatoes would grow stronger and yield a better harvest if I sowed and planted at the correct lunar phase.

After I poured a fifteen-liter jug of expensive extra-virgin olive oil, fresh out of the oil mill, into one liter bottles, I learned the hard way that I should never bottle during a waxing moon. Guido, another Tuscan friend, was sitting in the kitchen, having just finished trimming our trees during the waning moon. All of a sudden, one bottle after the other exploded. He helped me clean for two hours; then he explained what the waxing moon had to do with this slippery catastrophe. (His explanation can be found on page 89.)

Piece by piece, my treasure of practical experience increased. In the process, I learned to listen—really listen. When my teenage daughter started to have pimples, I called Carmen, whose cosmetic salon in Munich I had patronized for many years, to perform an acne treatment on her. "As soon as possible, please!" I said, "Jessica is desperate!"

I was astounded when Carmen replied, "It would be best to wait another week. Next Monday, we'll have a waxing moon.

Then, the blood will flow freely through the skin. I will be able to remove the pimples much easier and without scarring."

Our family doctor, who is knowledgeable in natural healing, suggested that our son's overdue tonsillectomy should not be done when the moon was in Taurus, because complications could easily occur. My dentist, who is interested in astrology, asked me to come in for my root canal on a day during the waning of the moon when—allegedly—it wouldn't hurt so much. (It didn't seem to make much difference.)

I found my hairdresser in Siena by chance. He took one look at my thin hair and said, "Next time you must have a haircut when the moon is in Leo. Then your hair will grow much stronger."

No wonder I wanted to know more about this topic! I began to study old and new books, farmer's almanacs and calendars, astrology books, and astronomy charts. I discovered that knowledge of the mysterious forces of the moon is ancient. For thousands of years, farmers—as well as healers, scientists, gamblers, lovers, warriors, poets, calendar makers, herbalists, and charlatans—used the ever-constant moon cycle for their purposes.

I must admit that not all the rules that have come down through the ages are correct. Some seem to be rather farfetched, at least at first glance, and many are pure superstition. Those that are most reliable, because they are the best documented, are the Moon Rules for agriculture. It is more plausible, for example, that your tomato plants will not germinate under the wrong lunar phase than it is that you will encounter a werewolf at the next full moon, as our medieval ancestors believed. Just as it is certain that the full moon will appear in the sky every 29 days, 12 hours, 44 minutes, and 2.8 seconds, it is also certain that the moon will influence people, animals, and plants in much the same way it rules the tides.

At one point, I started to write down according to subject the Moon Rules I had learned. Compiling notes on the Moon Rules has been a custom among farming families since the Middle Ages. Farmers also took note of recipes, herbal mixtures, and other important family traditions. Such chronicles were often recorded, like the family tree, on the blank pages of the family bible. I, however, only kept a record of Moon Rules. Whenever I found out that one of the rules worked, I would check it off in my private chronicle.

One day, my German publisher, Gerhard Riemann, called me. He wanted to know if I was interested in the moon, and wondered if I would consider writing a book about it… .

Here is the result: Moon Rules from a few thousand years, waiting for you to place a check mark next to those that work for you.

Why does the moon have such a definite influence on everything that happens on earth? Many convincing theories have been developed to explain this phenomenon. A few of the most important are presented in the chapter on the Moon and Science. We should not fool ourselves, however, by confusing fact and theory. Still, we can benefit from the experience that has been gathered. After all, most of us don't hesitate to switch on a computer or an iron without knowing exactly how electricity works.

Even skeptics can be convinced that certain vegetables will sprout better if planted during a waxing moon than if planted during a waning moon—except for onions, carrots, potatoes, and a few other species that yield underground. (More about this on pages 31 to 38 and 57 to 62.) Everyone with even the slight power of observation can see the connection between the moon and fertility in humans and animals. The fact that some rules are contradictory does not negate the moon's power over fertility cycles.

Similarly, I know that, in some areas, the new moon is considered to be the best time to ward off warts. Nevertheless, I will stick with my method. Jam, however, I will only cook during a waning moon. After all, I know what I know.

Part I

Gardening According to the Moon

Moon Gardener, International

Not everyone who has a green thumb is a good gardener.
Some have simply been sloppy with paint.

Not even the greatest skeptic can deny the relationship between the lunar phase and the growth and development of plants. No definite scientific explanation exists for this, which makes it more difficult for skeptics to accept. But facts are facts. This is not a question of belief or superstition, but of ancient experience collected over thousands of years. Many generations of farmers and gardeners did not understand anything about astrology, nor did they have any interest in it, yet they automatically considered the lunar phases—and often the signs of the zodiac, as well—in their work.

A very successful gardening book, first published in the United States in 1906 and revised every year since then, is the *Organic Gardening Almanac* (Llewellyn Press). Gardeners and farmers can refer to this book for the correct timing for all important tasks, such as planting, sowing, fertilizing, trimming, harvesting, and much more. Not only is the *Llewellyn* a best-seller in the agricultural world, it has also become a bible for those who love their gardens.

A similar but simpler version is *The Baccelli,* which has become popular in Italy. Before the end of the year, every tobacco store and newspaper stand sells the little blue moon calendar *Guida dell'Agricoltore*, which contains the lunar phases for the coming year, the dates for solar and lunar eclipses, and times that the moon will rise and set. Before beginning work, all farmers and everyone who works a plot of land—consult the *Baccelli* to see if the moon is *buona* or *non buona* at planting time. Most of these people have not heard about moon astrology, nor do they want to know about it.

Only in Germany have the old rules been forgotten over the past decades. The sowing calendar by Maria Thun has been in print for fifty years, but its sales volume cannot be compared with that of such folk almanacs as *Baccelli* and *Llewellyn.* Thun's calendar only remains popular among students of biodynamics and other "insiders."

Recently, however, moon calendars and almanacs for gardeners have popped up in many bookstores. These may confuse readers because there are three different kinds:

1. Some moon calendars only mention the four lunar phases. In most of these, the beginning of the new moon phase (referred to in this book as the first quarter) is symbolized by a black, round moon face. A sickle that opens to the left stands for the waxing moon, or the first quarter (referred to here as the second quarter. The beginning of the full moon phase (referred to here as the third quarter) is symbolized by a white moon face. A sickle that opens to the right stands for the waning moon, or the last quarter (referred to here as the fourth quarter).

2. Other moon calendars mention the lunar phases as well as the daily signs of the zodiac through which the moon is passing.

3. Yet other moon calendars and almanacs mention not only the lunar phases and signs of the zodiac, but also list gardening activities that are appropriate for a particular day.

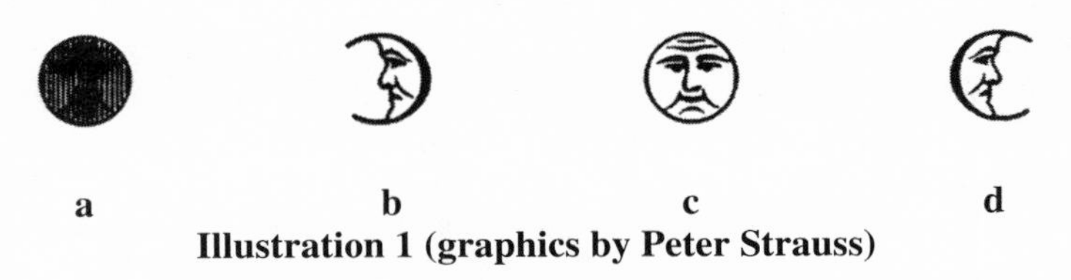

a b c d

Illustration 1 (graphics by Peter Strauss)

Simple moon calendars are sufficient for farmers and gardeners who have worked all their lives according to the moon and who know exactly what to do during each lunar phase. However, beginners who are interested in gardening according to the moon do not know how to use such calendars, and laymen who are unfamiliar with astrological terminology cannot use a moon calendar listing the signs of the zodiac through which the moon passes. Beginners need exact instructions about which activities to pursue during the various lunar phases. For example, when should one sow sunflower seeds? When should one trim apple trees, roses, and wisteria? When should one plant onions and crocus?

Weekend gardeners can find this information, along with many other facts, in the many work calendars for the gardening year that are currently on the market. Each day's entry gives the lunar phase and the zodiac sign through which the moon is passing. In addition, the best gardening activities are listed for that specific sign. Sometimes a symbol is all that indicates a suggested task. For example, a leaf might stand for leaf days—days that are best for sowing leafy green vegetables such as spinach, chard, and kale. A fruit might represent fruit days. A root might symbolize root days. So far, so good!

Comparing the different calendars with each other can be confusing. Various types of calendars list different dates for the signs of the zodiac. In one calendar, you may find the moon in Cancer, while in another it has already passed into Leo. Cancer is a fertile water sign, which is ideal for planting, while Leo is a fire sign, which is unfavorable for planting. A gardener who just learned this may wonder, "Which calendar is correct?"

Two ways to calculate the moon's position—the astrological method and the astronomical method—are both correct.

Astrologers use the earth as the center of the universe (geocentric). Their calendars place the moon in the sign of the zodiac where we would see it from earth. Astronomers base their calculations on the sun as the center of the universe (heliocentric). They provide the exact constellation (i.e., zodiac sign) through which the moon is passing at a particular moment.

About two thousand years ago, the astrological signs and astronomical constellations were matched. However, since the vernal equinox gradually shifts, these two systems now differ by about thirty degrees. As a result, geocentric and heliocentric positions can differ by as much as four days.

Illustration 2

Did you know?

The Moon Month Can Be Calculated in Different Ways

The monthly lunar orbit differs in length depending on the method of calculation. The synodic lunar month counts the time between two full moon phases as exactly 29 days, 12 hours, 44 minutes, and 2.8 seconds.

The sidereal lunar month is a little bit shorter: 27 days, 7 hours, 43 minutes, and 11.5 seconds. It is based on the background of the fixed stars and counts the time span the moon needs to return to a certain position on its orbit around the earth. The starting point of an orbit refers to the moon's passing before a first-magnitude fixed star—either Regulus in Leo, Spika in Virgo, or Antares in Scorpio.

Geocentric or Heliocentric: Which Method is Correct?

Technical information on these two methods is provided on page 266. Most gardeners, however, are less interested in complicated astronomical patterns and more interested in the question: "Which method is correct?" An even more pragmatic question would be: "Which method is most effective?" This issue has a history of raising controversy. Each side can show data and experimental results that demonstrate the superiority of their favored method.

Rudolf Steiner based his gardening theory on the heliocentric system. The sowing calendar of Maria Thun as well as the activities of biodynamic gardeners follow Steiner's philosophy. Without a doubt, this work is successful under specific conditions. However, even biodynamic gardeners admit that they can only sow and plant in really well-cultivated soil if they follow to biodynamic rules. Plants and soil do not respond to subtle energy influences after chemical fertilizers and insecticides have been in them for long.

Another disadvantage of the heliocentric system is that it can appear complicated to the layman. Besides the constellations, other factors that must be accounted for include the trine, apogee, and perigee (the farthest and nearest points of the moon's ellipses around the earth); lunar and solar eclipses; and the descending and ascending moon (not to be confused with waning and waxing of the moon).

Traditional gardening according to the lunar phases and astrological signs is much simpler. The beginner can skip the astrological signs if these seem too complicated and simply stick to the lunar phases. Since a glance up to the clear sky is the easiest practice, I have based this book on this classic method.

Anyone who wishes more detail can consult an ephemeris, which catalogs the moon's positions in the zodiac and is generally used to construct astrological moon calendars. Even better, consult *this*

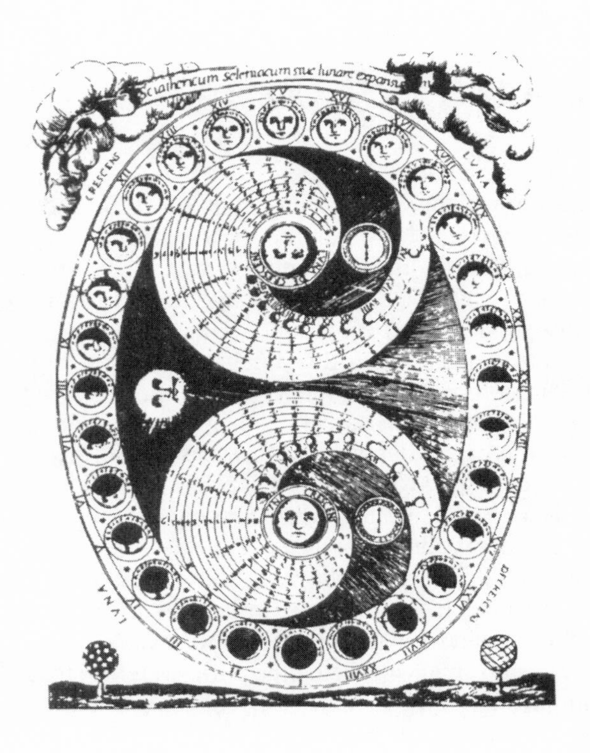

Illustration 3 (Graphics by Peter F. Strauss)

book! (The moon tables for 1996 to 1999 are on pages 275 to 311.)

Don't Forget the Green Thumb!

The Moon Rules are easy and have been proven over thousands of years. Nevertheless, for a variety of reasons, they will not suit everyone's garden.

In addition to the position of the moon, success in the garden is influenced by the fertility of the soil, weather, climate zone, and other necessities. The most accurate application of the Moon Rules will not be effective if the soil does not have enough nutrients or if it is too cold for sowing. The ideal date to turn the soil according to the moon calendar is not relevant if the ground frost is still six inches deep. The moon's position can only suggest a garden activity if the weather plays along!

Equally important, when it comes to gardening is *how*. A soil rich in humus, well cared for, and preferably without chemical fertilizers is still the final word in gardening. Astrological moon gardening enthusiasts must keep in mind that common sense, experience, gardening skills, and the famous green thumb are as important as the moon signs and phases. However, if all these factors have been taken into consideration, then the Moon Rules are the final touch that can make the difference between success and failure.

An understanding of esoteric philosophy is not needed to realize that the ancient hermetic principle "as above, so below" also applies to the garden. If a garden is treated according to astrological tradition, the plants will grow strong and bloom profusely even without chemical fertilizers. The fruit trees will yield an abundant crop, and tomatoes will taste the way they should. Above all, the gardener will have the very tangible benefit of having drawn a little closer to nature.

The Moon Phases

When you see the full moon poised in the sky, you can be sure of one thing: the moon will decrease a little bit more each day until, in about fourteen days, it disappears from the sky for a few nights. After that, it will increase for the next two weeks. After 29.5 days, a new full moon will rise. To be more exact, this occurs in 29.5309 days, or 29 days 12 hours, 44 minutes, and 2.8 seconds. This time span between two full moon phases will always be the same as long as the moon exists. Scientists refer to this process as "lunation," "a synodic month," or "a lunar cycle." Throughout the year, the moon makes this journey twelve times. Because the twelve cycles are completed in 354 days, the lunar phase shifts eleven days in the following year.

The fact that the moon continually changes its face within this cycle is the result of the relationship between earth, sun, and moon. While the moon circles around the earth, it reflects the sun's light (it does not have its own light) in different degrees according to the angle between sun and moon, as seen from earth. This cycle is usually divided into two to four phases. However, astronomy works with eight phases and astrological psychotherapy recently came up with 28 phases, or one per day.

Don't worry: we will only consider four phases. These can be enough to create confusion for the moon gardener because they sometimes go by different names. *New moon, first quarter, full moon,* and *last quarter* are the traditional names usually used in calendars. However, these terms can easily be misunderstood because the *first* quarter moon really marks the *second* quarter of the cycle. In order to avoid this confusion, we will only speak of the first, second, third, and fourth quarters.

The first quarter begins when the sun and moon are in conjunction. This means that the moon is between the earth and sun. During this time, for a few nights, it shows us its unillumined backside. Viewed from earth, this is the *new moon.* Other names for it include the dead moon and the dark moon. At the beginning of the first quarter, the moon is invisible. Toward the end of the first quarter, however, it appears shortly after sunset as a thin white sickle in the night sky. In gardening, the first phase signals new beginnings and sprouting.

The second quarter begins approximately seven days after the new moon, halfway between new moon and full moon. At this time, the sun and moon stand at right angles (90 degrees) to one another. This half moon rises around noon in the southern sky and sets around midnight. The second quarter signals the growth and development of whatever was started during the first quarter.

Sun-Moon Angle	**Terminology in this book**	**Other Terms**	
		two-phasic	*four-phasic*
after the conjunction			
0-90 degrees	first quarter	waxing	new moon
90-180 degrees	second quarter	waxing	first quarter
180-270 degrees	third quarter	waning	full moon
170-360 degrees	fourth quarter	waning	last quarter

The third quarter begins with the full moon, fourteen to fifteen days after the new moon. Because the sun and moon now oppose one another, the sun's light can shine upon the whole moon. The full moon rises at sunset in the eastern sky and shines throughout the night. The third quarter brings maturity and the ripening of fruit.

The fourth quarter starts about seven days after the full moon, when the sun and moon again stand at an angle of 90 degrees to one another. The waning moon rises around midnight. It is visible during the second half of the night and is poised above the southern horizon at sunrise. Two to three days before the new moon, its thin white sickle can be seen for the last time. After that, the moon is hidden for four to five days. The fourth quarter is a phase of withdrawal, decay, and tranquillity before another new beginning.

Did you know?

When Is the Moon at which Position in the Sky?

During a lunation (the period from new moon to new moon), the moon rises between fifteen and ninety minutes later each evening.

During the first days after the new moon, it is invisible. Toward the end of the first quarter, it appears as a thin sickle in the evening sky and disappears before midnight.

In the second quarter, the moon rises at noon and sets after midnight. It is visible during the first half of the night. At sunset it is poised above the southern horizon.

In the third quarter, the full moon is visible in the eastern sky at sunset and shines throughout the whole night.

In the fourth quarter, the moon rises around midnight and is visible during the second half of the night.

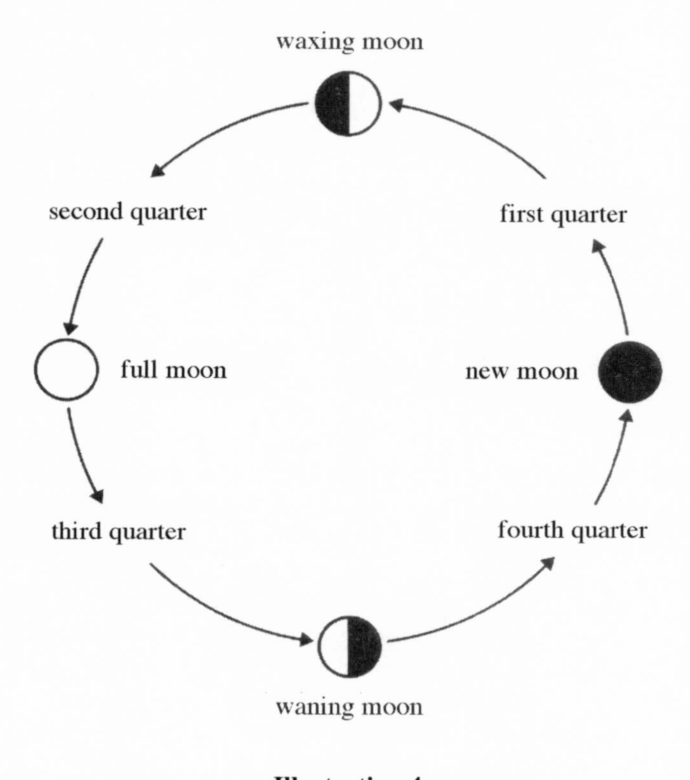

Illustration 4

The Moon Rules

Many Moon Rules for garden work to be performed in each of the lunar phase are hundreds—even thousands—of years old.

Some famous Greek and Roman philosophers, poets, and historians wrote down Moon Rules, although these should not be considered more correct than rules from the oral tradition. At the time of Homer, the Greek poet Hesiod wrote a verse known as "Everything on the Moon Phases," which gives the ideal time for nearly everything—from the date of sowing wheat to that of breeding of sheep. The Roman consul Cato recorded that one should plant fruit trees (figs, apples, pears, and olives) at the new moon, preferably in the afternoon without a southern wind. "The moon feeds oysters and fills the sea urchin and provides meat in fish and animal." The Roman satirist Lucilius wrote this sentence in 100 B.C.; even modern fishermen and butchers have nothing to add.

Pliny the Elder, another famous Roman, wrote an often quoted theory on brooding hens that is still practiced by some farmers: for healthy, strong chicks, only put eggs under brooding hens during a waxing moon. My Tuscan friend Fiorenza had never heard of Pliny the Elder (nor of Pliny the Younger, his writer nephew, for that matter) but she has bred her chicks according to his rules for as long as she can remember.

These classic authors have not remained famous for two thousand years on the basis of their agricultural expertise; thus, we can assume that they only recorded the knowledge of their day. By the way, the Celts were an excellent source for Pliny. Their customs and traditions gave him the material for the thirty-seven volumes of *History of Nature*.

Such writings are unusual, however. Most of the Moon Rules have been passed down from generation to generation by peasant families. For example, certain days are considered good (or bad) for sowing, cutting wood, breeding animals, and making wine. These rules, drawn from years of experience, were considered common knowledge.

Of course, a little superstition was added to these practical observations over the years. For example, one should only cut wood in December, on a day of the week without an "r." Some of our Tuscan village farmers still believe that a cow can only conceive when a farmer has led her to an open field where a bull awaits her under the full moon. This quaint superstition must bring tears of longing to the eyes of our poor cows who must endure artificial insemination in a stall.

Historically—the above mentioned and other doubtful facts aside—knowledge of the lunar phases was considered a serious and highly respected subject. Every farmer who took pride in himself knew these rules by heart; he knew exactly what work he had to do under a waxing or a waning moon. Although some of these rules only apply to certain regions with specific climates and soil conditions, many are more generally valid for our climate. If you want to try gardening according to the moon, you can choose among three different, but complementary, methods. You can choose one or two, or can even combine all three.

Gardening According to Two Moon Phases

Only two moon phases can be applied in the garden: the waxing and the waning of the moon. This is the simplest method that is most useful. My neighbor Walter Mehnert, who gardens in the middle of the city Munich, has worked with these two moon phases for sixty years. He declared, "Moon Rules must be very simple. Otherwise nobody has enough time to consider them." The farmers in our Tuscan village say the same. My girlfriend Neda and her father Amerio only distinguish between a "good moon" and a "bad moon." Whether the moon is good or bad, only they know. I have to milk an answer from them through persistent questioning. A good moon (e.g., for planting) can also be a bad one (e.g., for weeding). Hundreds of centuries of observation have reinforced the simple technique of looking up at the sky; anyone who thinks this is too simple should take a look at Amerio's vegetable garden.

The old-time gardeners say, "With the waxing of the moon, the earth exhales." When the sap in plants rises, the force first goes into the growth above ground. Thus, you should do all activities with plants that bear fruit above ground during a waxing moon. With the waning of the moon, the earth inhales. Then, the sap primarily goes down toward the roots. Thus, the waning moon is a good time to sow plants that bear fruit underground; it is also a good time for pruning, multiplying, fertilizing, watering, harvesting, and controlling parasites and weeds.

Gardening According to Four Moon Phases

The four moon phases offer a finer means of differentiation. The *Llewellyn's Moon Sign Book*, which I mentioned earlier, also recommends this method. An advantage of this relatively uncomplicated method is that you can make better use of the moon's effect. Experienced farmers know that one sows and plants leafy vegetables that yield above ground, as well as summer flowers and roses, during the first quarter. In the second quarter one sows and plants beans, tomatoes, peppers, squash, annual summer flowers, and berry bushes; one can also pick mushrooms at this time (preferably during the full moon). In the third quarter, one plants whatever bears underground. In the fourth quarter, one cultivates the soil and controls parasites. Anyone who cannot memorize these rules can consult the charts in the gardening section. With practice, you need only look into the clear sky to know the moon's position. Those who want to be more precise can look at the moon calendar on page 275 to 311.

Gardening According to the Signs of the Zodiac

The division into twelve signs of the zodiac is the most subtle of the three methods. Looking into the sky will not do the trick with this method; you must know in which sign of the zodiac the moon stands. A calendar is necessary for this. You can use the position of the moon in the signs successfully without astrological knowledge, but a basic knowledge of astrology contributes to better understanding.

The Zodiac

An ancient astrological rule states that each day of the month is influenced by one of the twelve signs. This is the basis for gardening according to the signs of the zodiac. The moon passes through these signs in a cycle and remains in each sign for about two and a half days. The zodiac starts with Aries and ends with Pisces. In each sign, the moon reflects the specific characteristics linked to that sign. You can use these qualities when gardening.

According to classic astrology, the signs fall into the following categories.

Day and Night Signs

- Masculine signs alternate with feminine signs.
- Day signs are masculine, active and dry. The day signs are Aries, Gemini, Leo, Libra, Sagittarius, Aquarius.
- Night signs are feminine, passive, humid, and fertile. The night signs are Taurus, Cancer, Virgo, Scorpio, Capricorn, Pisces.

Main Signs and Subsigns

There are cardinal signs, fixed signs, and mutable signs.

- Cardinal signs are at the beginning of a new season. They are active and lively. The cardinal signs are Aries, Cancer, Libra, and Capricorn.

- Fixed signs strengthen the influence of the previous sign. Therefore, they may be rigid, persevering, and a little stubborn. The fixed signs are Taurus, Leo, Scorpio, and Aquarius.
- Mutable signs follow the fixed; they may be changeable, capricious, unsteady, pessimistic, and unreliable. The mutable signs are Gemini, Virgo, Sagittarius, and Pisces.

Fire, Water, Air, and Earth Signs

These four elements compose the universe. Rudolf Steiner established a relationship among the four elements and the parts of a plant: seeds (fruit), blossoms, leaves (stems), and roots.

- Fire signs are hot, and therefore support the development of seeds and fruit. The fire signs are Aries, Leo, and Sagittarius. Days with the moon in these signs are the fruit days.
- Air signs are dry and promote blooming. The air signs are Gemini, Libra, and Aquarius. Days with the moon in these signs are the flower days.
- Water signs are humid and growth promoting; they are good for stems and leafs. The water signs are Cancer, Scorpio, and Pisces. Days with the moon in these signs are the leaf days.
- Earth signs have both feet on the ground; they are close to the earth, tough, solid, and promote root growth. The earth signs are Taurus, Virgo, and Capricorn. Days with the moon in these signs are the root days.

These observations and extensive experience gathered over the years eventually led to classification according to each of the twelve signs. A specific influence occurs in nature when the moon stands in one of these signs.

Moon in Aries

Rather infertile and dry, Aries is ruled by mars and influences the formation and maturation of seeds. Thus, it is a good sign for harvesting. It is also appropriate for digging, hoeing, and weeding. The Aries moon is unfavorable for sowing and planting. This is not disastrous for gardeners in the Northern Hemisphere because the waxing moon is only in Aries between January and March, a time when only the owners of greenhouses or cold frames are likely to start sowing.

Moon in Taurus

Taurus is a fertile, feminine earth sign ruled by Venus. In a Taurus moon, it is favorable to plant and sow. It is an especially good time for those plants in which strength goes into the roots and tubers. Cabbage and other leafy vegetables also benefit during this period. The Taurus moon is good for transplanting because the seedlings grow effortlessly and become robust, strong, and rather short plants.

Moon in Gemini

The ruling planet of heavenly Gemini is Mercury. During this rather infertile, dry sign, it is inadvisable to sow, with the exception of winding and climbing plants, because the plants have a tendency to become long, thin, and weak. The Gemini moon is very good for cultivating the soil and for harvesting. If you mow a lawn during this sign, the grass will grow more slowly and you can keep the mower in the shed for a while longer.

Moon in Cancer

Cancer is a cardinal water sign ruled by the moon. It is humid and fertile, which makes it ideal for sowing and planting. Sprouting takes place without any problems and young seedlings grow extremely quickly because this sign promotes stem and leaf development. Cancer moon days are also good for irrigating. If you water mainly on these days, the plants will absorb water most efficiently, thus saving water. This is also true for fertilizing.

Moon in Leo

Leo is a fire sign ruled by the sun. It is aggressive, masculine, hot, and the most infertile of all twelve signs. On Leo moon days, you should neither sow nor plant. Nearly all seedlings transplanted during a Leo moon wither. Instead, you should mow your lawn, weed, and pull out plants and shrubs that you wants to get rid of. Mowing in a Leo moon lasts even longer than in a Gemini moon. Weeding in a Leo moon in August will definitely get rid of unwanted plants.

Moon in Virgo

Mercury rules Virgo, which is an infertile sign, even though it belongs to the earth group. Thus, it is best to avoid planting vegetables on these days. However, annual summer flowers and climbing plants grow especially fast and produce many blossoms if sown or planted during a Virgo moon. This is a good planting sign if you want to cover a fence, arbor, or ugly wall with flowering clematis, honeysuckle, or climbing roses. Otherwise, take care of the soil and weeds on these days. You will also succeed in controlling aphids, snails, and other parasites in a Virgo moon. Preferably do this with natural means, without chemicals.

Moon in Libra

Libra is a cardinal air sign ruled by Venus. Moon gardeners consider it to be fertile and good for sowing and planting. Blossoms and flowers especially benefit from a Libra moon because Libra is the sign of beauty and aesthetics. Roses planted in a Libra moon—and of course cared for properly—are unbeatable in their beauty and strong blooms. Most vegetables develop well when sown in the sign of Libra.

Moon in Scorpio

Scorpio is a water sign ruled by Pluto. It is the most fertile sign, after Cancer, and is suitable for the same gardening activities. Flowers, vegetables, fruits, and berries all develop in abundance. The most outstanding characteristic of Scorpio is resistance. Perennial and herbaceous plants are extremely robust and winter-resistant if planted in a Scorpio moon. Thus, if your heart goes out to a special plant species that has a poor chance of surviving the winter, its odds can be increased if you plant it in a Scorpio moon. Nevertheless, be sure to cover such plants for the winter.

Moon in Sagittarius

Sagittarius is a fire sign ruled by Jupiter. This can be a good opportunity to either harvest or cultivate the garden. The Sagittarius moon is quite unsuitable for sowing and planting because it is rather dry and infertile. Nevertheless, Sagittarius stimulates the development of fruit and some moon gardeners use this time to plant apple and other fruit trees. If there is no time to garden on a more favorable day, you can also plant carrots, onions, and potatoes, but make sure that the moon is waning.

Moon in Capricorn

For moon gardeners, Capricorn days are semi-fertile. Capricorn's ruler is the strict Saturn. It is an earth sign, good for planting vegetables that yield underground, such as potatoes, carrots, beets, and onions. Because Capricorn influences the roots, trunks, and bark, ornamental shrubs, bushes, and trees planted in a Capricorn moon also have a good chance. Try not to plant flowers on Capricorn days.

Moon in Aquarius

Aquarius is a very dry air sign. Its ruling planet is the austere Uranus. It is best to do such garden work as digging, weeding, and pest control in an Aquarius moon. Stay away from sowing and planting and the other more creative garden activities. Only onions and pine trees, which are ruled by Uranus, can endure planting during an Aquarius moon.

Moon in Pisces

The last sign of the zodiac is humid and fertile, almost as fertile as Cancer and Scorpio. Its ruling planet is Neptune. Plant and sow as you like to, because almost everything flourishes in a Pisces moon. This is an especially suitable time to plant root vegetables and flowers that grow from bulbs and tubers. Herbaceous plants and bushes have especially deep root systems and promise the greatest success when planted in dry soil in a Pisces moon.

Because information on the signs of the zodiac is more than anyone can digest at a time—not to mention memorize—you can look up the best time for various garden activities, as needed.

Cultivating the Soil

Heaven is as much under our feet as above our heads.

Henry David Thoreau

Not even plants can exist on air, love, and lunar phases alone, although these are important requirements for any development. Plants, of course, also need water, sun, warmth, and a fully nourishing soil. The right planting mix provides more than a dozen nutrients, the most important of which are nitrogen, phosphorous, and potash. In addition, plants will not grow without the so-called ten secondary nutrients and trace elements. Indeed, each plant needs everything—only in different proportions.

Unfortunately, an ideal soil for all agricultural purposes does not exist. Like humans who have different nutritional habits, depending on the geographic area in which we live, so do plants. Rhododendrons, for example, require acidic soil because they originated in the wooded areas of the Himalayas and grew accustomed to that type of climate. Roses, on the other hand, require an abundance of potash, having become accustomed to that in their Asiatic homeland. Some plants are picky when it comes to their nutrition. For example, sunflowers are real gluttons, gorging themselves on all the nutrients their roots can take in. Other plants are undemanding, almost ascetic, and yet others are gourmets. Some love cozy, warm mulch covers, while others prefer to sleep uncovered.

All this information is important for gardeners because plants are moody and react sensitively if one ignores their wishes. Knowing this, humans have tried for thousands of years to make their stay in our gardens as comfortable as possible. Unfortunately, we cannot influence some things, such as the sunshine. However, we can help in other ways, especially with respect to the soil. Few garden owners are lucky to find a fertile, balanced soil. Most soils show major deficiencies. The most frequent problems that gardeners face are:

- soil that is too heavy or too light
- soil that is too acidic or too chalky
- soil that has a miserably thin humus layer

Once we have figured out where the problem lies, we can solve all three of these conditions. Today, we can find this out easily by going to a garden center and buying a test kit to analyze the condition of the soil. Soil that is too heavy can be lightened by adding sand; chalk can be added to acidic soil; and clay powder can be added to give more substance to light soil. The optimal time for these activities is during a waning moon. Then, as farmers say, the earth breathes in and is ready to absorb the soil-improving additives.

Good soil conditions, however, are not sufficient. We must constantly replenish the nutrients that plants extract from the soil. For a long time, common belief was that we could easily remedy such deficiencies with chemicals. Artificial fertilizers and chemical pesticides promised to guarantee great harvests with little effort. Today, more than a hundred and fifty years after the invention of chemical fertilizers, we have the results: huge flowers without brilliance or fragrance, apples and tomatoes with no taste, harmful substances and heavy metal deposits throughout the soil, and parasites that resist nearly everything.

Many of us have returned to the old methods in order to reestablish a natural balance in the earth. According to astrological principles, substance is never lost; it is only transformed. Thus, we recognize that it is essential to return the nutrients that we have removed; to give back to the earth the fruits we have taken from her. The best route to revitalize exhausted and leeched soil passes through the compost heap.

Composting Made Easy

Not long ago, people smiled indulgently on gardeners who put their kitchen garbage in a compost heap or asked a farmer for some cow manure. In recent years, composting has gained in popularity due to ecological concerns. Much of what has been written about the fine art of composting makes it seem extremely complicated. In reality, however, the recipe for preparing home-made humus is simple.

You only need air, water, some soil, plant matter, and, if available, rotten manure. Every household yields an abundance of organic kitchen garbage, including potato peelings, tea leaves, raw fruit, and vegetable stalks. Gardens yield plenty of material suitable for composting: dead leaves, weeds, clippings from hedges, dead flowers, and human, and animal hair. Although meat and fish remnants could be used, these attract unwanted visitors from the animal kingdom; thus, it may be more advisable to throw them into the garbage can.

Garbage can be transformed into compost through the work of soil dwellers and microorganisms that live underground. Billions of these creatures can be found in each handful of soil. Since the beginning of time, these 'underworlders' have done their job even without help. However, you can speed up the process of composting by giving them a little assistance.

Compost for Beginners

First choose a garden plot that is in semi-shade and not too far from the kitchen, so that it will be just as easy to take the garbage outside as it would be to guiltily toss it into the garbage can. Next, choose a compost box from among the many varieties available. Although some types are better than others, any one with enough ventilation and direct contact with the ground will do the job.

Throw only organic garbage into the compost box. Fill it eight to twelve inches high and then sprinkle a layer of manure, lime, and bone meal to quicken decomposition and create the best compost. If the compost is too dry, add water until it is as moist as a squeezed sponge. Then sprinkle a little garden soil over it, and perhaps also a layer of bone meal. Repeat this process over again, layer after layer, until the entire box is full.

The compost is ready when it has turned into a brown, crumbly soil that smells like forest earth. If you follow the above rules and do nothing else, the compost will be ready in about half a year. If the weather is warm, it will ripen even faster.

The lunar phases influence the composting process. Start composting during a waning moon, preferably in the fourth quarter. Under the most ideal conditions, the moon should be in Cancer, Scorpio, or Pisces. Avoid using undiluted compost for sowing or for planting seedlings because it has a very high level of nutrients. Nearly all types of garden beds will welcome a thin sprinkling of compost that is raked in loosely during a waning moon. These include flower and vegetable beds, branch stumps on fruit trees, and berry bushes. If you can afford the luxury, also spread it on the lawn, preferably in the autumn. In all other cases, the ideal time to give the compost back to the earth is spring, during the waning moon in March and April. This is also the best season to start composting.

What Do I Put into the Compost?

You can put the following into your compost box:

- Coffee filters, tea leaves, eggshells, vegetable ends (leaves and stalks), and fruit leavings.
- Wild herbs, dead flowers, weeds (first discard the seeds), lawn cuttings (in small amounts), dead leaves, hedge and tree cuttings (chopped into small pieces), and used soil.
- Sawdust, blank paper (in small amounts), straw, animal and human hair, and wood ashes.

What Should I Not Put into the Compost?

Do not put the following into your compost box:

- Stone, glass, metal, printed paper, cleaning aids, sewage, meat, coal ashes, and plants with chronic diseases.

Today, interestingly, composting is more widespread in urban than in rural areas. When I asked my Tuscan friend Neda when and how she made up her compost, I only got a blank smile. "*Composto?* What is that?"

Of course, I thought that I had used the wrong word. Perhaps the Italian word for compost was something completely different. I began to explain: "To compost you use potato peelings, fruit leavings, spoiled fruit, and old vegetables."

She looked at me dubiously and said, "These we feed to our chickens and rabbits. From there, it goes to the plants. Diluted with water, chicken and rabbit manure is an excellent fertilizer."

> ***Did you know?***
>
> *The Champion of Roots*
>
> A single leguminous, sown for green fertilizing, produces about one and a half miles of roots every day. In one season, this would form a train track one hundred and fifty miles long. And this is not counting the tiny hair roots! Include them, and the track would be about 3,000 miles.

Green Fertilizing

Another effective method to improve the soil is green fertilizer made from living plants. For weekend gardeners, this method is only useful when a plot of land has lain fallow for a long time; for instance, when building a new house. However, even in a well established garden, green fertilizing can work miracles in tired beds. Green fertilizing loosens hard-packed soil and provides it with an abundance of nitrogen, which is necessary for growth.

Lupine, lucerne, peas, green beans, shamrock, mustard, phacelia, and spinach are especially valuable as nitrogen sources. Sow these plants during a waxing moon. Cut them just before they bloom and turn them under the hungry soil. Always spread green fertilizer and turn it under the soil during a waning moon, preferably in the fourth quarter on water days (Cancer, Scorpio, and Pisces).

To Turn or Not to Turn?

Beginners at organic gardening still argue whether or not it is better to till the soil in autumn, or if it is sufficient—or even gentler—to simply loosen the soil with a tilling fork. Today, the suggested technique is to loosen the soil carefully so that the microorganisms are not disturbed. These underworlders have a hard job transforming organic garbage into humus. If their working place becomes too cold or too dry, or is disturbed, they go on strike.

In the autumn, no matter what, loosen up the soil during a waning moon and enrich it with compost and organic fertilizer. Allow it to freeze in big clumps. In the spring, use your cultivator to turn up the soil for aeration and add compost and organic fertilizer to replenish it. Finally, use your tilling fork to break it into crumbs.

Rule of Thumb:

Four Inches of Compost Make Eight Inches of Healthy Soil.

Always cultivate the soil during a waning moon, preferably in the fourth quarter and in the signs of Gemini, Leo, Virgo, and Aquarius.

Table 1

Soil Treatment According to the Moon

Activity	*Moon phase*		*Quarter*	*Zodiac sign*	***Season***
	Waxing	Waning			
Bring out compost		X	3, 4	Cancer, Pisces	Spring, fall
Sowing for green fertilizer		X	4	Cancer, Scorpio, Pisces	April till end of August
Start the compost		X	4	Cancer, Scorpio, Pisces	All year
Turn, loosen, improving, soil (when the earth thaws)		X	3, 4	Aries, Gem, Leo, Virgo, Aqua	Spring
Weeding		X	4	Aries, Virgo, Leo, Sag	as needed
Working in the green fertilizer		X	4	Cancer, Scorpio, Pisces	6-10 weeks after sowing

Sowing and Planting According to the Moon

There is a time... to plant...

Ecclesiastes 3:1-2

Seeds seem to know exactly when to start growing. It is as though they possess an inner computer that registers temperature, humidity of the soil, and the influence of light—and gives the starting signal at the right moment. Most seeds have a programmed dormant phase that can last up to several years. Some have a hard shell that offers protection and gives them warmth during the winter. When a seed gets the signal to sprout, it allows moisture to penetrate its shell until it swells and bursts open. Then sprouting can begin.

Unfortunately, seeds know more than do weekend gardeners. Often, the latter cannot wait until spring for sowing. When spring arrives late and the snow does not want to leave the beds, weekend gardeners can use a bit of cunning and sow seeds in cold frames or sprouting boxes on a windowsill. This fools the seed into believing it is already spring.

The risk-free time for sowing outdoors requires a judgment call. It is certainly wiser to wait until the soil is warm and dry, and night frosts are over. Ancient garden wisdom says that plants sown late, when the soil is warm and dry, make up for their delayed start. However, most 'passionate' gardeners cannot wait until that time. Fortunately for these impatient people, there are vegetables and flowers that are not sensitive to cold and can survive a minor frost. Under favorable circumstances, such plants can come outdoors earlier.

Hardy Vegetable Species:

The following can be planted early:

- Potato, chervil, cress, leek, mangel-wurzel, parsley, radish, red beet, lettuce, salsify, spinach, and onions.
- From April on, also plant perennial herbs such as mugwort, lovage, horseradish, melissa (balm), and pimpernel. Only do so when the soil is dry, free of frost, and a little warmed up. Without a minimum of warmth, even the hardiest plants will not develop.

Delicate Vegetable Species

After the middle of May sow or plant the following species:

- Eggplant, beans, cucumbers, squash, corn, melon, peppers, and zucchini.

Did you know?

A Starting Signal for the Gardening Year

An old farmer's rule gives a clear-cut way to tell when you can start on the garden beds: when the dirt clods don't stick to your boots anymore.

Summer Flowers

- Many annual summer flowers are safe for planting outdoors beginning in March, but for sure in April. Mallow, Clarkia, cosmos, California poppy, cornflower, marigold, annual larkspur, baby's breath, sunflower, and sweet pea are some examples.
- Especially robust species, such as marigolds, can go into the ground during the previous autumn. In this case, they will bloom a little earlier.

How Do I Sow?

If the soil is dry, water the area for sowing a day ahead. Either sow in single rows or furrows, or scatter the seed over a general area. Sowing in rows has the advantage that all seeds lie at the same depth. With a hoe, plow a furrow half an inch deep and drop a few seeds in at regular intervals. Sow the seeds far enough apart so that the seedlings will not need separating later. Cover the seeds with soil. Remember: cover—not bury! Tamp the soil carefully with the flat side of a hoe. In dry weather, moisten the freshly planted bed with a fine mist. Continue to keep the bed moist.

If sown too closely together, plants will need thinning so that they do not suffocate each other. There should be four to six inches between each plant. Even if you find it hard to do so, leave only the strongest plants. Pull the rest carefully, which is easiest when the soil is damp. You can give away the thinned plants, or transplant them in another area of your garden.

Did you know?

Reduced Sprouting Time

You can reduce the sprouting time of seeds by soaking them in a cup of tea for at least three days. This convinces the seeds to believe that it is already much later than they thought, and they sprout faster. Shortly before the full moon, most seeds sprout the fastest.

Sowing According to the Moon

In addition to the season, seed quality, and soil temperature, the moon is very important for sowing or planting so that vegetables, herbs, and flowers develop well. Moon Rules make no distinction between sowing and planting. I haven't found a farmer's rule anywhere that does not refer to both sowing and planting.

My friend Neda, however, claims that only the date of sowing is important. She says that, if the gardener from whom I buy tomato plants has sown in the wrong lunar phase, my tomatoes will not develop well, despite my best efforts. Although I believe nearly everything Neda says because I know her garden, I am not sure whether she is correct on this particular point. However, Neda does agree with all the other moon gardeners that the waxing moon is good for sowing or transplanting most plants.

Sowing According to Moon Phases

In the Waxing of the Moon (first and second quarter)

Plant everything that bears fruit above ground, especially annual plants, during a waxing moon. This type of vegetation only lives through one season; you must resow it the following year. Most summer flowers and vegetable species belong to the annual group. Vegetable types that bear above ground include tomatoes, broccoli, zucchini, and peas.

In the Waning of the Moon (third and fourth quarter)

During a waning moon, put into the earth biennials, perennials, and bulbs as well as vegetables that bear underground. Biennials are flower species sown in the spring that bloom in the summer of the following year. Examples include delphinium, pink, and stock. Perennials (also called herbaceous) are blossoming plants that come up several years in a row. Examples include aconite (monk's hood), bell flowers, marguerite, larkspur, crane's bill, and phlox. Root vegetables bear their edible parts underground. Examples include carrots, radishes, potatoes, and onions.

The following rule of thumb is valid for sowing:

- At the waxing of the moon, everything that bears above round.
- At the waning of the moon, everything that bears underground.

In addition, you might consider the appropriate sign of the zodiac.

- Best: moon in Cancer, Scorpio, or Pisces.
- Quite good: moon in Taurus, Capricorn, and Libra.
- Unfavorable: moon in Virgo and Sagittarius
- Very unfavorable: moon in Aries, Gemini, Leo, and Aquarius.

It is reasonable to combine lunar phases and the signs of the zodiac. When choosing a method for planting or sowing, the lunar phase is most important. Of course, there is always the risk of planting on an infertile day.

Rule of Thumb

For the Sowing and Planting of Annual and Summer Flowers

- Libra moon for beauty
- Cancer, Virgo, or Pisces moon for abundance of blooms
- Scorpio moon for endurance
- Taurus moon for robustness

Sow all in the first quarter.

Where there is a choice, there is a struggle…

—German proverb

Sow all flowers with filled blooms (for example, marguerite, stockgarden, balsam, and peony) during a waxing moon whether they are annuals or herbaceous plants.

In the Flower Garden

Flowers from Bulbs and Tubers

There is no clear-cut answer to the gardener's question: "When do we plant bulbs for spring and summer flowers?" This means dahlias, freesias, gladioli, anemone, ranunculus, crocus, tulip, narcissus, and many more.

"Of course, plant them during a waxing moon," Neda says. In principle, it is best to plant or sow flowers during the waxing moon. As do most Tuscan people, Neda sows even biennials during a waxing moon. I tend to believe her. Each year in May, I stand in amazement before her meadow full of thousands of wild, white-orange blooming daffodils. Every year there are more. Her dahlias are twice as high and large as everyone else's, including mine.

According to the Moon Rules, bulb and tuber flowers, which are rhizome plants, should be treated like vegetables and, therefore, be planted during a waning moon. This is supposed to put power into the bulb. The Llewellyn calendar recommends that flower bulbs be planted during the third or fourth quarter (i.e., a waning moon), preferably on a fertile Cancer, Scorpio, or Pisces day. Elsewhere, it is suggested that crocus, tulips, narcissus, and other bulb flowers go into the ground during the moon's first or second quarter, preferably in Virgo or Libra.

Perhaps the solution is that some gardeners dig up their flower bulbs every year and store them in the cellar until next season, while others leave them in the earth. Neda never digs up her bulbs (e.g., crocus, narcissus, and tulips) because she wants them to multiply. She also leaves her dahlias in the ground because the mild climate of Tuscany makes digging up unnecessary.

Try to plant early bloomers (e.g., crocus, winter aconite, spring star flower, wild tulips, and snow drops) during a waning moon so that they will later grow strong daughter bulbs. Dig up large bulb plants (e.g., hyacinth, tulips, and dahlias) after they have bloomed. These need replanting during a waxing moon. Newly bought bulbs have all the nutrients the plant needs for blooming, already stored in the bulb for that season. They begin to gather the nutrients for the next season after blooming. When these wonderful bulbs have finished blooming, you have two choices.

- Throw them on the compost (this would be wasteful, of course).
- Fertilize them intensely during a waning moon. You can do this while they are still blooming. Then wait until the leaves die back. Dig up the bulbs and tubers during a waning moon, preferably during a fertile sign (i.e., Cancer, Scorpio, or Pisces). Store them in a cool place and replant them during a waxing moon of the next season.

Did you know?

Flower Bulbs for Naturalizing

Plant bulbs in the second quarter for early bloomers. To grow to an entire carpet of narcissus, crocus, and snowdrops, plant flower bulbs during the third quarter. If digging them up, do so during a waning moon, preferably in Cancer, Scorpio, or Pisces.

Table 2

Times for Sowing in the Flower Garden

Species	*Moon*		*Quarter*	*Zodiac sign*
	Waxing	*Waning*		
Aconite		X	3	Cancer, Scorpio, Pisces
Alyssum		X	1, 2	Cancer, Scorpio
Annual flowers	X		1, 2	Cancer, Scorpio, Pisces, Libra
Aster		X	1, 2	Virgo
Bellflower		X	3	Cancer, Scorpio, Pisces
Biennial flowers		X	3, 4	Cancer, Scorpio
Bulbs & tubers for volunteering		X	3	Pisces, Scorpio, Cancer
Bulbs & tubers for wintering	X		1, 2	Libra, Virgo
Carnation	X		1, 2	Cancer, Virgo, Libra
Chrysanthemum	X		1	Virgo
Coreopsis	X		2	Libra
Cosmos	X		1, 2	Libra
Cranesbill		X	3	Libra
Crocus		X	3, 4	Virgo
Delphinium		X	3	Libra
Gladiola	X		1, 2	Libra, Virgo

Species	*Moon*		*Quarter*	*Zodiac sign*
Herbaceous in general		X	3	Cancer, Scorpio, Pisces
Honeysuckle	X		1, 2	Virgo, Scorpio
Hyacinth		X	3	Cancer, Scorpio
Iris	X		1, 2	Cancer, Virgo
Larkspur, annual	X		1, 2	Libra
Larkspur, herbaceous		X	3	Cancer, Scorpio
Lily	X		1, 2	Cancer, Scorpio
Marguerite, annual	X		1, 2	Libra
Marguerite, herbaceous		X	3	Cancer, Scorpio
Marigold	X		1, 2	Cancer, Scorpio
Narcissus	X		1, 2	Virgo, Libra
Narcissus, wild		X	3, 4	Cancer, Virgo, Libra
Nasturtium	X		1	Libra, Cancer, Scorpio, Gemini, Virgo
Peony	X		1, 2	Virgo
Petunia	X		1, 2	Virgo, Libra
Phlox		X	3	Cancer, Virgo, Libra, Scorpio
Pinks		X	3	Cancer, Scorpio
Poppy	X		1, 2	Virgo

Species	*Moon*		*Quarter*	*Zodiac sign*
Portulaka	X		1, 2	Virgo
Rose	X		1, 2	Cancer
Strawflower	X		1, 2	Cancer, Scorpio
Summer sage		X	3	Cancer, Scorpio, Pisces
Sunflower	X	X	2-4	Libra
Sweetpea	X		1, 2	Cancer, Scorpio
Trumpet flower	X		1, 2	Cancer
Tulip	X		1, 2	Virgo, Libra
Tulip, wild		X	3, 4	Libra, Virgo
Wallflower		X	3	Cancer, Scorpio
Winding & Climbing plants		X		Virgo, Gemini
Zinnia	X		1, 2	Libra

Climbing Plants

Climbing plants improve the appearance of ugly concrete walls, give privacy from curious onlookers, and provide shade. They need a support (i.e., at least a fence) to cling to, lots of fertilizer, and the correct planting date. Winding and climbing plants that are primarily for blooming, do well planted in a Gemini moon, and even better in a Virgo moon. In the sign of Virgo, they get a strong, tall vine or stalk, expand quickly, and soon provide shade; their blooms will be abundant, but their fruits will not. Honey suckle is one of the climbers that grows especially fast.

Plant climbing plants that bear a harvest (e.g., beans, cucumbers, squash, and yellow squash) during a waning moon in Pisces so that their fruit will be at its best. If height and a privacy screen are the objective, the shoots will grow longest in Scorpio.

Annual climbing plants with lovely flowers include fire pod, Japanese hops, morning glory, star vine, nasturtium, black-eyed Susan, and sweetpea.

In the Vegetable Garden

Sowing According to the Moon Phases

In the first quarter, during a waxing moon, plant vegetables that bear above ground and that have external seeds. These include cauliflower, endive, cabbage, kohlrabi, butter lettuce, cress, Brussels sprouts, celery, asparagus, spinach, and zucchini.

In the second quarter, during a waxing moon, sow and plant vegetables that bear above ground and have fruit with internal seeds. These include eggplant, beans, peas, squash, peppers, and tomatoes.

In the third quarter, during a waning moon, sow and plant mainly root vegetables. These include carrots, potatoes, garlic, horseradish, parsnip, parsley root, radishes, white radish, red beet, salsify, celery root, and Jerusalem artichoke. Also plant biennials (e.g., strawberries) and leafy vegetables that must not go to seed too early (e.g., butter lettuce, spinach, and leek).

In the fourth quarter nothing should be sown.

Here Are Some Exceptions that Prove the Rule

- Encourage the first spring vegetables (e.g., lamb's lettuce) to grow faster by sowing during a waxing moon, preferably in the first quarter.
- Sow butter lettuce during a waning moon (third quarter), otherwise it goes to seed.

- Carrots are root plants and should be sown during a waning moon. If they seem to grow too slowly, stimulate growth by sowing during a waxing moon.
- Cucumbers are plants that carry their seeds in the fruit; thus, they should be sown during the second quarter. Because the cucumber is the diva of the vegetable garden, it appreciates special treatment. It develops best when sown or planted in the first quarter.
- Sow peas during a waning moon, otherwise they bloom without forming pods.
- Beans develop best when the moon is full at sowing time.

Did you know?

Good Friday Potatoes

My Tuscan neighbor Gastone always plants potatoes on Good Friday. Why? He does not know. "Tradition," he says, shrugging his shoulders. His father and grandfather always did the same. The explanation is simple. Easter is always on the first Sunday after the first full moon following the vernal equinox. Good Friday is two days earlier. This means that he usually plants potatoes during a waning moon, exactly as the Moon Rules prescribe.

For those who regard these rules as too complicated, the following table gives the sowing dates for a vegetable garden.

Table 3

Sowing and Planting in the Vegetable Garden

Species	*Moon*		*Quarter*	*Zodiac sign*
	Waxing	Waning		
Artichoke	X		1	Cancer, Pisces, Virgo
Asparagus			3	Cancer, Scorpio, Pisces
Beans	X		2	Cancer, Scorpio, Pisces, Libra, Taurus
Belgium Endive		X	3	Cancer, Scorpio, Pisces
Broccoli	X		1	Cancer, Scorpio, Libra, Pisces
Brussel sprouts	X		1	Cancer, Scorpio, Pisces, Libra
Butter lettuce		X	3	Cancer, Scorpio, Pisces, Libra
Cabbage	X		1	Cancer, Scorpio, Pisces, Libra, Taurus
Carrots		X	3	Taurus
Cauliflower	X		1	Cancer, Scorpio, Pisces, Libra
Celery root	X		1, 2	Cancer, Scorpio, Pisces

Species	*Moon*		*Quarter*	*Zodiac sign*
Cress	X		1	Cancer, Scorpio, Pisces
Cucumbers	X		1	Cancer, Scorpio, Pisces
Eggplant	X		2	Cancer, Scorpio, Libra
Endive	X		1	Cancer, Scorpio, Pisces, Libra
Garlic		X	3, 4	Scorpio, Sagittarius
Green onions	X		2	Cancer, Scorpio, Sagittarius
Horseradish	X		1, 2	Cancer, Scorpio, Pisces
Kohlrabi	X		1, 2	Cancer, Scorpio, Pisces, Libra
Leeks	X		2	Sagittarius
Okra	X		1	Cancer, Scorpio, Pisces, Libra
Onions		X	3, 4	Taurus, Libra, Pisces
Parsley	X		1	Cancer, Scorpio, Pisces, Libra
Peas	X	X	2, 3	Cancer, Scorpio, Pisces, Libra
Peppers	X		2	Scorpio, Sagittarius
Potatoes		X	3	Cancer, Scorpio, Taurus

Species	*Moon*		*Quarter*	*Zodiac sign*
Radishes		X	3	Libra, Taurus, Pisces
Redbeet roots		X	3	Cancer, Scorpio, Pisces
Rhubarb		X	3	Sagittarius, Taurus
Runner beans	X		1, 2	Cancer, Scorpio, Pisces
Rutabaga		X	3	Cancer, Scorpio, Pisces
Sage		X	3	Cancer, Scorpio, Pisces, Sagittarius
Spinach	X		1	Cancer, Scorpio, Pisces
Squash	X		2	Cancer, Scorpio, Pisces, Libra
Strawberries		X	3	Cancer, Scorpio, Pisces
Tomatoes	X		2	Cancer, Scorpio, Pisces Libra, Sagittarius
Zucchini	X		2	Cancer, Scorpio, Pisces, Libra

Did you know?

Leeks Can Be Divided

Although you may prefer to plant leek seeds, you can also buy leeks with viable roots in the supermarket. Plant these during a Sagittarius moon in the second or third quarter. At blooming, many little daughter bulbs divide off (i.e., as garlic does). Plant these also during the second or third quarter of a Sagittarius moon. Leeks taste best and have the most delicate flavor during the spring.

Did you know?

Seeds at their Best

The American moon gardener George Llewellyn developed a recipe for home-grow pedigree seeds. This is the perfect mixture of seeds, gathered over three years.

Sow each mother plant during a specific moon sign. Sow the seed from the first year during the first quarter moon in Cancer to ensure fertility. Sow the seeds of the second year during the first quarter moon in Libra to ensure beauty. Sow the seeds of the third year in the first quarter moon in Taurus to ensure endurance.

You can combine qualities, as needed. Good growth of roots comes in Pisces; endurance and new growth come in Scorpio, as do endurance and resistance to drought. Other combinations are also possible. Of course, this only works with real seeds, not hybrid seeds.

In the Fruit Garden

Planting Trees, Shrubs, and Berries According to the Moon

Compared with the complicated rules for sowing flowers and vegetables, planting trees and shrubs is easy. Plant trees and shrubs during a waxing moon in the second quarter, in a fruit-fertile sign (i.e., Cancer, Scorpio, or Pisces). This applies whether they are ornamental or bear edible fruit and berries. The same is true for climbing plants, such as blackberries and raspberries, or vines. In case you miss the second quarter, the third quarter is not too late for planting.

> ***Did you know?***
>
> *Long-Lasting Christmas Trees*
>
> Even in heated rooms, Christmas trees will keep their needles longer if cut in December three days before a full moon. At this time, most of the moisture is in the trunk. However, this advice does not help you much if buying a tree at a Christmas tree stand. It only works if you cut your tree at a tree farm, or at least select it there. The tree will last for a surprisingly long time.

In the Herb Garden

Sowing According to the Moon

In several chapters, this book is concerned with herbs, especially in relation to health and beauty. Herbs are also mentioned in the chapter on moon magic, which outlines the moon's influence on the soul.

The original uses for most herbs were to heal diseases, for magic rituals, and to spice food. Herbs have been equally successful in all these areas. For centuries, people had no other means to accomplish these purposes. The healing and magic effects of herbs are fascinating and can be understood, at least in part, by the lunar phases during which they are sown and harvested.

All herbs, of course, have different requirements regarding soil, light, temperature, moisture, and nutrients. The most favorable time for sowing and planting is the same for all. Regardless of their use (e.g., spice, beauty, healing, or magic) the waxing of the moon is the right time. The first or second quarter is best, preferably in the fertile signs of Cancer, Scorpio, and Pisces.

You can develop almost all annual and perennial herbs from seeds. Often it is advisable to buy them in the nursery as seedlings. Of course, this gives you no control over the time of sowing, but at least you can transplant the young herbs at the best time.

Did you know?

Hostile Herbs

Herbs are ideal for cultivating a mixed garden. Most of them are undemanding and are not as picky about their neighbors as are many vegetables, which can become sick if they do not like their neighbors. However, some herbs do have definite problems with other plants. For example, caraway does not get along with coriander. Parsley does not go with lettuce. Sage does not like celery. Mugwort, lovage, and wormwood do not cohabit well with any neighbor.

Loving Care Until You Can Harvest

More plants die from too much fussing than from neglect.

Sorry, but I have to say it: seedlings will not grow by themselves, even if you provide a nutrient-rich soil and pay attention to the right lunar phase for sowing. On the contrary! It is then that the real work begins. Your vegetable, fruit, and flower plants need cultivating, nurturing, feeding, tying on supports, and freedom from nasty weeds and dangerous parasites. Luckily, the moon can help you select the right time to make watering, weeding, pruning, fertilizing, and exterminating parasites less work and more successful. This is even true for the unpopular task of lawn mowing.

Watering

One thing is for sure. Most weekend gardeners not only water more often than necessary, but they give their plants more water than they can take. For the gardener, it may feel comfortable and relaxing to stand with a hose over the plant beds. He might think he is making his plants happy but, in reality, he does not please them at all.

In the normal rhythm of nature, plants learn to be economical with their allotment of water. If there is a lot of rain, they satisfy their thirst. In longer dry spells, however, they make an effort to extract the last drop of moisture from the deeper layers of the earth. This forces them to grow deep root systems. As a result, they become stronger and more resistant. If the gardener appears with his hose at the end of a hot summer day, the plants come to rely on his regular supply. Their roots remain shallow, growing near the surface of the well-watered soil. For this reason, you should only water when needed.

Plants enjoy having the soil surface loosened with a tilling fork once a week during periods of drought. This allows air to penetrate the soil. Of course, it is much harder work than watering. I know what I am talking about. A year ago I planted one hundred and fifty-nine trees in a small olive grove in Tuscany. When I am in Munich, my neighbor Guido takes care of it.

During a hot spell last summer, Guido came by just as I was trying to add three hundred feet to my hose so I could water the future orchard.

"Forget about the hose," Guido said. Instead he put a *zappa* (hoe) in my hand. "If you begin watering, then you will have to keep doing it."

Again he was right. However, I had to loosen the dry, stone-hard soil around one-hundred and fifty-nine young trees! I can tell you I really felt it in my back.

If regular watering of a garden has already begun, of course, it cannot be abruptly stopped. Even so, plants can gradually become accustomed to less water. Eventually, they will only need it during an extreme drought. In the transitional period, make sure that plants get the minimum amount of water necessary, but do not let them get thirsty. Water dilutes the nutrients in the soil so that plants can absorb them through their roots. If the plants do not get enough moisture, they dehydrate and starve.

By the way, plants can also sweat. Not only does the soil evaporate water, the plants evaporate it as well. The moisture they lose in this process has to return to the soil. In our climate zones, nature takes care of this cycle through rain and dew.

Nature only needs support when it does not rain for long periods of time. Using either a simple hose or a complicated sprinkler system, water thoroughly, regularly, and abundantly. Frequent—but insufficient and irregular—watering harms plants more than one can imagine. Sporadic watering creates black spots on tomatoes. If you use the hose regularly but quit too soon, plants with deep root systems may not get any moisture.

Most experts are of the opinion that early morning and early evening are the best times for watering. However, other methods should be considered as well; for example, sprinkle the earth and leaves in the early morning, before 9:00 A.M. If there is a problem with fungus in the garden, avoid watering the leaves and irrigate only the soil. The best time for this would be between 1:00 and 3:00 P.M., when the sun is high in the sky. Do not water after 3:00 P.M. in order to keep fungus at a minimum. If you experiment with both possibilities, the plants will reveal which method they prefer.

According to astrology, there is no debate about the best days for watering. The moon is the ruling planet over water. Thus, the best days are when the moon is in a water sign (i.e., Cancer, Scorpio, and Pisces). If necessary, a Libra moon is also possible. The most effective time is when the moon is waning, because then the soil breathes in and can profit most from watering. For this reason, less water is actually more. Scientific experiments have confirmed this ancient farmer's wisdom. Repeated and strictly controlled lab tests achieved consistent results showing that beans absorb the most water under a full moon, and the least under a new moon.

Fertilizing

Plants will not feel satiated even though they have good, nutritious soil and enough water (always on water days, that is). Without quick remedial action, they simply stop growing. In addition to good soil and water, as well as light and warmth, they need twelve nutrients for development. Even the best humus has only a small part of what is necessary. Foremost among these requirements are nitrogen, phosphorus, and potash. Nitrogen is for high growth and lush green leaves. Phosphorus stimulates the growth of blossoms and fruit. Potash provides plant roots with strength. They also need calcium, iron, magnesium, sulfur, copper, chlorine, and several other trace minerals.

Plants derive the three most important nutrients primarily from the soil. Because they need high amounts during growth periods, the supply of nutrients in the soil needs replenishing from time to time. Good cultivation of the soil is just not enough; plants need fertilizer in order to produce more flowers, beauty, and fruit.

A Rule of Thumb

That Has Proven to Be Very Good

Root vegetables (e.g., carrots, white radishes, and beet roots) and fruit vegetables (e.g., tomatoes, peppers, zucchini, and cucumbers) need fertilizer that contains a little more phosphorus and potash. Leafy vegetables (e.g., lettuce, spinach, and cabbage) need a little more nitrogen.

Be careful with nitrogen-rich fertilizer. Tests have shown that the level of nitrogen in our gardens is usually higher than necessary—and also higher than is good for us. Therefore, test the soil before fertilizing. If hungry plants still need more nutrients, avoid chemical fertilizers. Use organic fertilizers (e.g., blood meal, bone meal, or guano) instead because they work more slowly, allowing the nutrients to reach the roots through the soil, and are milder than chemicals.

Although mineral fertilizer works faster and is cheaper than organic fertilizer, it has tremendous disadvantages. It not only increases the salt level of the soil but can also harm the "ground crew" living underground (i.e., organisms that enrich the soil). Minerals leach into the ground water and, in contrast with organic material, do not improve the soil.

Organic fertilizers usually originate from animal by-products, primarily horn meal and blood meal (rich in nitrogen), and bone meal (rich in phosphorus). Only farmyard manure has enough potash. The fertilizer industry mixes organic power cocktails from these three main nutrient groups for nearly every purpose. It is difficult to make a mistake if one follows the directions.

Farmyard manure, on the other hand, is not as foolproof. Although this excellent fertilizer has proven itself over thousands of years, it can trigger mass death in a vegetable bed if it is too fresh when added to plants. If you are lucky enough to get fresh farmyard manure—which has become very rare—be happy. However, first put it on the compost, where it will lose its pungency, so that it can be of more use later.

When Do I Fertilize?

When fertilizing, you should also first consult the moon calendar. This time, however, it is easy because the rules are the same as with watering. All days that are appropriate for watering are equally good for fertilizing. These are Cancer, Scorpio, and Pisces days, preferably during a waning moon in the third and fourth quarter.

Perhaps you have a good reason to make an exception and use a chemical fertilizer. In such a case, the Llewellyn Moon Calendar suggests using it during a waxing moon in the first or second quarter. At this time, plants will consume it most sparingly because the earth is breathing out, and therefore absorbs less fertilizer.

Spread green fertilizer in the fourth quarter during a waning moon. Work it into the ground during the same lunar phase.

If you are in a hurry for some reason to transplant seedlings on a specific 'fast growing' moon date. During the first and second quarters, you may prepare the soil with a fertilizer (e.g., a finely powdered blood meal, which is highly effective). Then, if the seedlings shoot up and need extra food, the soil has already absorbed this strengthening cocktail.

Did you know?

A Cow-Friendly Hay Harvest

An old farming rule said never to fertilize a meadow while the moon was in Libra because the cows would not eat the hay.

Plants with Hearty and Weak Appetites

Not all plants have equal appetites. Some are real gluttons; others are extremely undemanding. In gardening, we usually classify plants as heavy, medium, or light consumers.

Heavy consumers need regular, generous helpings of compost and organic fertilizer (e.g., guano, blood meal, bone meal, lime, and fermented plant water).

Medium consumers feel satisfied with compost and an occasional handful of fertilizer and a dollop of fermented plant water.

Light consumers are humility incarnate. They can live for a year on leftover fertilizer that the more demanding plants did not eat last summer.

A Miracle Cure—Stinging Nettle Water

Nobody really knows why, but if seedlings do not want to grow in spite of the best care, plant waters can work miracles. At unbelievable speed, they make plants strong, healthy, and very resistant to parasites. Here is a proven recipe:

Put a 15 to 30 gallon barrel of wood or clay or plastic (which should not contain chlorine, because chlorine ions harm plant water) in a shady place. Preferably on an Aries day, fill it with fresh stinging nettles that have not yet bloomed (blooming stinging nettles are not as effective). Fill the barrel up to the rim with water. Add a handful of organic fertilizer and cover it with a screen to prevent animals from falling in. Do not put a full lid on the barrel before the mixture has completely fermented. Stir vigor-

Table 4

Hearty Appetites	*Medium Appetites*	*Weak Appetites*
Artichoke	Beans	Azalea
Cabbage	Cucumber	Begonia
Celery	Dahlia	Chamomile
Chrysanthemum	Fennel	Cress
Corn	Gloxinia	Horseradish
Eggplant	Lettuce	Lamb's lettuce
Fruit trees	Silverbeet	Pansy
Geranium	Onion	Parsley
Leek	Peas	Peppermint
Potato	Peppers	Petunia
Rhubarb	Red beet	Primrose
Squash	Roses	Radishes
Strawberry	Spinach	Rhododendron
Sunflower	White radishes	Rosemary
Tomato	Zucchini	Sage

ously every day with a stick so that a lot of air can penetrate the brew.

After a few days, the contents will foam and stink. To control the strong odor, add a couple of handfuls of lime every day when you stir the plant water. This controls the smell and adds important minerals at the same time.

After about fourteen days, the plant water will be ready. The nettle leaves will have decayed and only the stems will be recognizable. Fish out the stems with a pitchfork and throw them on your compost heap. Diluting a quart of plant water with nine quarts of tap water will fertilize two to three square yards of garden bed. Apply this mixture to the garden during a waning moon once a week, preferably during a water sign, and watch the plants grow!

You can improve this basic mixture by adding two chopped onions, garlic greens, and a handful of healing herbs to the barrel of stinging nettle stew. Thyme, lavender, and rosemary, as well as many other herbs, are rich in essential oils if picked at the full moon.

Table 5

Let's Have a Good Neighborhood in the Garden!

Plants are like people; not all of them can get along with each other. The following table lists which ones like to live together and which do not.

Plant	*Friends*	*Foes*
Beans	Carrots, Cabbage, Cucumbers	Onions, Peas
Bush beans	Strawberries, Cabbage, Cucumbers	Fennel, Onions
Cabbage	Potato, onion, celery, sunflower	Strawberry, tomato
Carrot	Tomato, lettuce, peas, leek, onion, chives, dill	
Celery	Leek, bush beans	Corn
Corn	Beans, potato, peas, squash	Celery
Chives	Carrot	Beans
Cucumber	Beans, white Radish, Cabbage	Herbs, potatoes
Dill	Cabbage, Carrots	
Eggplant	Beans	
Fennel	Only flowers & herbs	Nearly all vegetables

Plant	*Friends*	*Foes*
Garlic	Rose, strawberry	
Leek	Carrot, celery	Beans, peas
Lettuce	Strawberry, carrot	Parsley
Onion	Red beet, strawberry, tomato	Peas, beans, potato
Potato	Beans, peas, cabbage	Sunflower, celery
Red beet	Onion, cabbage, lettuce	Wax beans
Squash	Corn	Potato
Tomato	Green asparagus, parsley, onion, carrot	Peas, red cabbage, potato
Zucchini	String beans, onion	

Pruning According to the Moon

There is a lot to trim in a garden: trees and shrubs, lawns and meadows, hedges and slips. Strange as it may sound, most gardeners have a healthy respect for pruning plants. The higher the tree, the more they fear making a mistake. Mowing the lawn is not usually a feared job, but it is also not a well-loved job. Let's start with the lawn.

Mowing

Even if nothing grows as expected, grass will. One can actually hear it grow. On an early Saturday morning, when the gardener wants to sleep in, the grass will grow to an offensive height, literally forcing him to get up and mow it. As attractive as a well-manicured lawn might be, it is also a burden. Can nothing make it grow more slowly? Yes! Some weekend gardeners claim that their lawns grow more slowly if they mow during a waning moon in the third or fourth quarter in a fire sign (Leo), or in Virgo or Gemini.

I have to admit that I know one case in which a lawn was mowed strictly according to Moon Rules. To the amusement of the entire neighborhood, it grew faster and stronger than ever. As far as I know, this was an exception. At least one can give the Moon Rules a try.

When grass is still very young, it should grow faster and stronger. In this case, mow it during a waxing moon (first or second quarter) under one of the water signs, Cancer, Scorpio, or Pisces.

Trimming Fruit Trees

Amateurish snipping away at fruit trees and shrubs can do more harm than good. There are only four reasons to prune a fruit tree.

1. Little trees sometimes need their fruit buds thinned so that they will not collapse under the weight of the fruit.
2. The tree has to be shaped to maximize light exposure to all the branches.

3. One must remove weak, damaged, or diseased wood.
4. Cutting back branches will stimulate the formation of fruit buds.

If one of these four reasons applies to a tree, the next question is when to trim.

Thinning, shaping, reducing fruit buds, and removing damaged branches are activities preferably performed in February when the hardest frosts are over. Always do this during a waning moon because there is too much sap in the trees during a waxing moon. Trimming trees is especially dangerous at the time of a full moon when sap runs easily and the trees lose all their energy.

The third or early fourth quarters with the moon in Sagittarius or Aquarius are ideal. The tree has the best chance for survival without shock, and for growing back healthy and strong. Some moon gardeners consider a fertile sign, preferably Scorpio, to be the best time. Such complications! I agree with my neighbor the old gardener who says, "Moon Rules must be simple, otherwise they are useless. I trim a few days after the full moon. It has always been good for my trees."

In general, the following rules are helpful:

1. Repair work and removing diseased and damaged wood is necessary as soon as one detects damage. Remember to do this during a waning moon.
2. Stimulate the growth of fruit wood by cutting back right after the blooming time, also during a waning moon and in a fertile sign.
3. To stimulate the growth of a sapling, trim a third of its branches in late winter, during a third quarter moon in a fertile sign. Repeat this procedure each winter for the first four years.

Did you know?

When a Fruit Tree Does Not Bear Fruit

If a fruit tree does not want to bear fruit any more, hammer a big nail into its trunk at 45 degree angle, just above the ground. Then the tree thinks that it is female and will bear fruit.
This ancient farmers' rule, which originated in Columbia, has been successfully practiced by old-time fruit farmers. I can only guess in which moon phase one should do this procedure. The tree would probably suffer less during a waning moon.

Pruning Roses

Prune back roses every year to make them look healthy and attractive and produce as many beautiful blooms as possible. Without pruning, the proud plant will soon look bald and mousy. Always use sharp pruning shears, otherwise the tool could crush the branches. Cut during a waning moon, just above one of the outward-pointing buds.

Did you know?

Prune Roses While Forsythia Blooms

When is the best time to prune roses? An old farmers' rule says, "In spring when forsythia is blooming." Do this during a waning moon, preferably in an air sign (i.e., Gemini, Libra, or Aquarius).

Bush Roses

Prune during a waning moon at the beginning of spring, just before budding. First remove the dead wood, then cut back any weak shoots and branches that have grown toward the middle. Shape the plant so that the branches end at the same height from the ground.

Climbing Roses

In the spring, remove all dead and weak wood. Trim the climbing shoots after flowering time, otherwise the development of blossoms will be stunted. Cutting after the plant has bloomed will stimulate new growth and encourage new side-branches that will bring forth flowers in the next year.

> ***Did you know?***
>
> *European Rose Balls: Where Do They Come From?*
>
> In former times, Farmers Balls, or Rose Balls were only available in certain parts of Europe. Today they are everywhere. These colorful glass balls are often very pretty. These days, their beauty is enough reason to have them around. In the olden days, they had another important job. They were called 'witch balls' because it was commonly believed that they protected plants from negative power, while they collected positive power from the sun and moon.

Trimming Hedges

Trim all hedges so that they can develop as many twigs as possible and become very dense. You can best achieve this by trimming them right after planting. All the experts agree on this. However, when is the best time to trim them afterwards? There are as many opinions about this as there are species of hedges—which suggests the comforting conclusion that just about any time is fine.

Trim evergreen and green hedges in spring and late summer. If a hedge flowers before the end of June, trim it as soon as it has finished blooming. This helps the plant form new blooming shoots at the lower trunk in the following year. After 21 June, trim hedges that bloom in the early spring so that they will not lose blossoms. Most flowering bushes, shrubs, and hedges bloom before the end of June, and therefore should be pruned in the same year.

The best moon phase depends on your intention. If you want a hedge to grow as slowly as possible, the best trimming time is during a waning moon, in the third or fourth quarter, preferably in a fire sign (i.e., Aries, Leo, or Sagittarius). If a hedge is still young and needs to grow fast and thick, I recommend trimming during a waxing moon in a water sign, preferably in Scorpio.

Pruning Slips

Most weekend gardeners have tried cuttings to propagate their balcony flowers, flowering or evergreen shrubs, and house plants. Nearly everyone has experienced at least one failure. It is like a curse!

Everything may be correct. The timing is right (i.e., while the plant is in full bloom). The slip cuttings have three to seven leaves, two to four inches long, right below the leaf node. All the blossoms and nearly all the leaves, except the lowest pair of leaves, were removed. The cuttings are safe in a little greenhouse, or under a plastic bag, in the right starting soil. And yet, not a single cutting grows!

This has happened even to the Munich gardener Walter Mehnert, who says, "One year, none of my geranium cuttings grew. Since then, I have returned to my old custom. I cut and plant my cuttings only during a waxing moon. Now, all of them flourish."

After four to six weeks, relocate slips that have formed roots in their own pots, filled with a mix of soil and turf. They can wait out the time until spring in a greenhouse or a bright, frost-proof room.

Plants that multiply well through cuttings include geranium, verbena, hydrangea, barberry, busy lizzie, liverwort, cotoneaster, box tree, treasure flower, fuchsia, and oleander.

It is also possible to make cuttings from berry bushes, roses, and other ornamental plants between October and the beginning of spring, preferably during a waxing moon in the sign of Pisces. Until they root, put them into damp sand or immediately plant them in soil, about 8 inches deep.

Cutting Vines

The best time for cutting vines is in the spring before shoots appear, in the third quarter of a Cancer, Scorpio, or Pisces moon. Then they grow best.

Parasites: Enemies in Your Garden Bed

Experienced gardeners are correct when they claim that pests and parasites have little opportunity to spread in a well-established garden that has been cultivated with organic methods. Some gardeners are so generous that they tolerate the intruders that sneak into their garden beds, reasoning that each parasite is useful—although not necessarily for the plants. Some contend that even gluttonous snails fulfill an important task. They are the trash men, so to speak, for rotten, organic leavings and little dead creatures. Of course, they can also carry away half the garden.

Most hobby gardeners hate these enemies in their garden beds and plan revenge. As understandable as this reaction may be, it is more reasonable to first determine why so many parasites and bacteria have attacked the garden. Is the soil lacking nutrients? Are there too many nutrients? Are the plants living next to the right neighbors? Maybe two are standing side by side that do not like each other—this happens with plants, too! Is there enough light for all of them? Are they standing in the right spot?

Experience has shown that prevention is the best means to keep plants healthy. Sometimes, however, even under the best conditions, parasites get out of hand and a war cannot be avoided. Nevertheless, one should attack the problem with focused intent. Use only those materials that destroy the parasites without harming such garden helpers as hedgehogs, ladybugs, and lacewings. Try getting rid of enemies with the help of astrology and other natural methods. If spraying chemicals is unavoidable, then pyrethrum preparations combine maximum usefulness with a minimum of damage. The ideal time for such procedures is during a waning moon, during the fourth quarter in an infertile sign (i.e., Aries, Gemini, Leo, Virgo, or Aquarius).

Sometimes a plant is ailing even though parasites are not detected and it appears to be getting enough nutrients and water. In this case, there is only one cure: destroy the plant before it can infect others. Throw it into the garbage can, never on the compost pile.

Did you know?

Demanding Cucumbers

Anyone who has planted cucumbers knows how picky they are. Gardeners will do just about anything to please this diva of the vegetable bed. Consequently, folk wisdom has countless rules regarding the planting of cucumbers. One of them says that, to protect cucumbers from pests, plant them before sunrise on May Day (1 May). Preferably, this should be done by a naked young man!

Recipe for Pest Control

Collect the harmful critters that make the plants miserable. If there is about half a cupful, smash them up with a mortar and pestle into as fine a mush as possible. Mix them with one quart of water. Shake vigorously. Pour the mash through a strainer into a glass jar with an airtight lid. Add a few drops of this extract into a spray bottle filled with water. Spray this onto the diseased plants. Store the remainder in a cool place. Respray once a week. The pests will withdraw with surprising speed.

Did you know?

The Second Harvest of Beans

My neighbor the gardener told me how to outwit my bush beans for a second harvest. Instead of uprooting his bean plants after the first harvest, he cuts them back to about four inches, waters them generously, and gives them an extra helping of organic fertilizer. The exact time is during a waxing moon in a fertile sign (i.e., Cancer, Scorpio, or Pisces). About four weeks later, he harvests fresh beans.

Did you know?

When Are the Forces of the Full Moon Most Effective?

Put plants into the soil a few days before the full moon for them to take advantage of its special powers. If you wait until the exact date of the full moon, the forces of the waning moon will have already begun.

This is true in reverse for the maximum advantage of a waning moon's powers.

Destroying Weeds and Undergrowth

Many moon gardeners believe that the optimal periods for eradicating weeds are while the sun is in Aries (around 20 March to 20 April), in Leo (20 July to 20 August), and in Sagittarius (20 November to 20 December) and the moon is in Aries, Leo, or Sagittarius, if possible during a waning moon. Weeds, undergrowth, and undesirable but stubborn plants pulled at this time have no chance. Other gardeners are convinced that a Gemini moon is ideal for permanent eradication of weeds and to prevent felled trees from growing back. However, Walter Mehnert says that it does not have to be so complicated. Pulling weeds during a waning moon, a few days after the full moon, insures that they will not return.

Table 6

Loving Plant Care According to the Moon

Activity	*Moon*		*Quarter*	*Zodiac sign*
	Waxing	*Waning*		
Cutting for stimulation		X	3	Cancer, Scorpio, Pisces
Cutting fruit trees		X	3	Sagittarius, Aquarius
Cutting slips and suckers		X	3, 4	Cancer, Scorpio, Pisces
Exterminating weeds		X	4	Aries, Leo, Sagittarius
Fertilizing		X	3, 4	Cancer, Scorpio, Pisces

Activity	*Moon*		*Quarter*	*Zodiac sign*
	Waxing	*Waning*		
Fertilizing for speedy growth	X		1, 2	Cancer, Scorpio, Pisces
Fertilizing with plant water		X	1, 2	Cancer, Scorpio, Pisces
Green fertilizing		X	4	Cancer, Scorpio, Pisces
Mowing for slow growth		X	3, 4	Leo, Virgo, Gemini
Mowing for strong growth	X		1, 2	Cancer, Scorpio, Pisces
Pest control		X	4	Aries, Gemini, Virgo, Leo, Aquarius
Pruning fruit trees		X	3, 4	Sagittarius, Aquarius
Pruning roses		X	3, 4	Gemini, Libra, Aquarius
Trimming hedges for slow growth		X	3, 4	Aries, Leo, Sagittarius
Trimming hedges for strong growth	X		1, 2	Scorpio
Watering		X	3, 4	Cancer, Scorpio, Pisces

Harvesting and Using

... and there is a time to harvest.

Ecclesiastes 3:2

For gardeners who have cultivated their soil, planted, watered, fertilized, controlled pests, and pruned according to the Moon Rules, it is natural to also pay attention to the moon when they harvest and conserve their fruit. You can call upon ancient traditions in this case as well. For thousands of years, long before the refrigerator and even preserving with sugar, finding a way to preserve the harvest was crucial to survival.

The rules for harvesting listed here are primarily for fruits and vegetables that need storing. If you intend to eat produce immediately, harvest it when it is as ripe as possible, preferably right before the meal. The aroma of fruit is most intense when it is ripe. Pick only as much as you can eat. During a waxing moon, fresh fruit perishes more quickly.

If one likes mushrooms, pick them after a rain. They can also be picked on full moon days, when they will be in abundance because the soil is moister.

Fruit and Vegetable Harvest

To store fruit and vegetables, you should process them first. It is advisable to pay attention to the moon. Produce keeps its flavor much longer, and is less perishable, if harvested during a waning moon in the third and fourth quarter. Fruit for preserving can be picked when it is still a little hard and unripe.

To harvest according to the signs of the zodiac, consider harvesting produce on warm, dry days under the fire signs Aries,

Leo, and Sagittarius, or on airy Gemini and Aquarius days. Produce will stay fresh and fragrant for a longer period of time.

Dig up seed potatoes on full moon days in January. For the harvest of root vegetables, the ideal time is when the sun is in the sign of Virgo or another earth sign.

A Few Harvest Hints that Have been Proven for Centuries

- Olives: a waning moon
- Mushrooms: the full moon
- Wine grapes: as close as possible to the full moon
- Grapes for raisins: a waning moon
- Fresh flowers that are supposed to keep long: a waning moon
- Beans & legumes for drying: a waning moon
- Potatoes for storing: a waning moon
- Seed potatoes: the full moon
- Healing and aromatic herbs (e.g., peppermint, thyme, melissa, lavender, sage, marjoram, oregano) for drying: the third quarter
- Root vegetables: in a fire or air sign in the third or fourth quarter
- Herbs, flowers, and fruit for drying: a waning moon
- Fruit for drying: a waning moon in a fire sign
- Comfrey, digging and processing for an ointment: a moon in Virgo or Capricorn
- Marigold, picking and processing for an ointment: a moon in Libra or Aquarius
- White radishes and horseradish: a moon in Scorpio
- To harvest vegetables: after the full moon
- Flavorful fruit: never in Scorpio

Herb Harvest

According to an old folk belief, nature receives special blessings between 15 August (Assumption of Mary) and 8 September (Mary's Birth). In former times, this was a big season for herb collectors. Even nowadays some villages celebrate the blessing of herbs at Mary's Assumption. People use the blessed herbs for healing or mix them with cow and horse feed on Christmas Eve or during the Twelve Nights of Christmas.

The Moon Rules and special rites and traditions of former times that pertain to the harvesting of healing and magic herbs are discussed in a later chapter on magic plants. At this point, we will only discuss the harvesting and drying of spice herbs.

Some herbs have flowers that can be harvested for drying. Cut them when the blooms have just opened. To harvest only the seeds, cut the bloom clusters when the seeds have started to turn brown. To dehydrate the roots, gather the herbs during a waxing moon, preferably just before the full moon, when they contain more moisture and are most tender. The time for maturation and blooming is the same for many herbs. The best time for harvesting herbs for drying is during a waning moon in the third quarter, when there is less moisture in the plants.

The morning of a sunny day is ideal. It should be late enough that the early morning dew has already dried, and early enough that the essential oils in the little pores and channels of the leaves, stems, and seeds have not yet dried. Dedicated herb collectors harvest between 10:00 and 11:00 A.M. Cut the herbs with a sharp knife and only gather what will be processed in the same day. Herbs that have been lying around for a while lose their aroma quickly. Gather the various herb species in different baskets so that their fragrances do not mix. Keep only the healthiest and most beautiful specimens. Only wash the herbs that will be dried if it is absolutely necessary. Afterwards, gently pat them dry with a kitchen towel.

All plants, including herbs, are more than 70% water. The art of drying is to remove the water as quickly and thoroughly as possible while preserving the oils. Best results come from drying in a dimly lit room at 70 to 80 degrees. Good ventilation is important so that moisture evaporating from the plants does not remain in the room.

If necessary, dehydrate the herbs in an oven. Turn it on at the lowest setting and prop the oven door open with a spoon or similar tool. Spread the herbs in a loose, single layer on a tray. Never dry herbs in the sun. Too much light and heat will evaporate the volatile oils. If the leaves crackle to the touch, the herbs are ready for storing. Most dried herbs will last for about a year.

The following herbs are especially good for drying: mugwort, tarragon, mint, sage, savory, marjoram, rosemary, and thyme.

A Few Rules for Preserving, Stocking, and Storing

- Jam, jelly, wine, 'must' (a wine product), and fruit preserved in alcohol should always be preserved during a waning moon. This way they last longer because fruit ferments slower than it does during a waxing moon. For jelly and jam, the best moon is during a fixed sign (i.e., Taurus, Scorpio, and Aquarius).
- Fruit and vegetables should be preserved during a waning moon in a water sign (i.e., Cancer, Scorpio, and Pisces).
- Dried fruit should be stored during a waning moon, preferably in a fire sign (i.e., Aries, Leo, and Sagittarius), also in Capricorn and Aquarius.
- Shred and pickle cabbage during a waning moon of Capricorn, Libra, or Sagittarius. When the moon is waxing, it ferments too quickly.
- Preserve root vegetables during the third and fourth quarter of a Capricorn moon.
- Bake during cardinal signs (i.e., Sagittarius, Cancer, Libra, and Capricorn). The dough rises higher and, during a waxing moon, the bread is lighter.
- Make wine and transfer it into bottles during a waning moon.
- Preserve vegetables preferably during a water sign.
- Open a barrel of must during a waning moon, otherwise it will be explosive.
- Do not store fruit during a Virgo, Aquarius, or Pisces moon because it will perish too easily.

- Do not put away geraniums and other potted plants that will winter indoors or in a cellar during a Virgo, Aquarius, or Pisces moon. They will perish faster this way.

Did you know?

When You Bottle, You Must Consider the Moon

My Tuscan friend Neda always knows a little more about the Moon Rules than other people do. She points out, "It is not important when tomatoes, olives, and grapes are harvested. It's much more important on which day or time you bottle wine, or olive oil, into *damegiana* (balloon-shaped bottles), or cook and jar *sugo* (tomato sauce), or jar jam. It really won't work during a waxing moon because the volume of wine or other preserves expands in the bottle and the level of liquid rises. Even wine can demonstrate this. Because wine expands during a waxing moon, the oil stopper that seals the wine in a vacuum will climb and sometimes even jumps out of the bottle.

"The same can happen with tomato sauce, as I have experienced myself. This also applies to oil and jam. Jam that is jarred at the waxing moon," Neda says, "ferments and becomes moldy. In *luna calante* (the waning moon), however, nothing can go wrong. Anyone who chooses not to believe this can see for himself that the wine level under the oil stopper sinks when the moon is waning."

Moon and Science

The day science begins to examine nonphysical phenomena it will make greater progress in one decade than in all the previous centuries of its existence.

Nicola Tesla

For thousands of years, people have observed that the Moon Rules regulate moisture and thus have a great influence on the growth and development of plants. Pliny, Aristotle, and Plutarch wrote about this. Stonehenge, built 2,000 before Christ, was a precise agricultural device to measure the sun's and moon's positions. It was used to figure the best dates for planting. However, only those scientists are interested in these historical facts that pose the question whether these ancient theories really work. If they do, the key question is how the moon influences the growth and development of plants.

Because the moon's influence is very subtle, and because research in this area does not earn ambitious scientists academic laurels, little significant research has been conducted. One of the few scholarly works in this field is from Professor F. Brown of Chicago. We have already mentioned his experiment with beans in the chapter on watering—remember? Even in a completely dark laboratory, his beans absorbed noticeably more water during the full moon than at new moon. The German botanist Dr. Lily Kolisko proved through her experiments that vegetables grown above ground develop especially well and have a good flavor when sown during a waxing moon— a fact that moon gardeners already know.

The results of experiments by American botanist Clark Timmins are also of interest. Under controlled conditions, he sowed different kinds of seeds (i.e., peas, tomatoes, marigold, and cosmos) during a waxing moon. Shortly afterward, they all sprouted. Moon gardeners would have expected this. Then he sowed the same seeds from the same bags during a waning moon. Many did not sprout at all, and those that did became miserable, little plants. Then he sowed tomatoes on a fertile water day (i.e., a moon in Cancer, Scorpio, or Pisces) and received a sprouting rate of 90%. The same seed sown on a Leo day (infertile) only had a sprouting rate of 58%. One hundred percent of tomatoes transplanted on a Cancer day started to grow, while only 6% of others transplanted on an infertile Sagittarius day grew. Tomatoes planted in the right sign bloomed 12 days earlier and gave more and better fruit.

Finally, Timmins sowed his tomatoes according to the fertile days mentioned in two different moon calendars. He was surprised to find that the tomatoes planted according to one calendar developed wonderfully, while those planted according to the other calendar developed miserably. He compared the dates carefully and discovered that the lagging plants had been sown and transplanted on a day that was a fertile Cancer day according to the heliocentric calendar but was an infertile Leo day according to the astrological geocentric calendar. This is a result that the followers of the geocentric model (which this book follows) like to quote.

Not quite as convincing are the results of an eight-year series of experiments published in 1990 by another scientist, Hartmut Spieß, who planted according to both geocentric and heliocentric methods. He used the sidereal and synodic, tropical and anomalistic moon orbit, apogee and perigee, and concluded that lunar phases influenced the growth of his radishes and rye, but that the condition of the soil and the weather played a far more important role. At first sight, these results may sound disappointing. Moon gardeners would probably agree, albeit begrudgingly. Nevertheless, even scientists no longer deny the correlation between plant growth and the moon's position.

The controversial question that remain is: why does this correlation exist, and what causes it? Light? Magnetism? Tides within the plants themselves? Scientists are pondering this, but so far no one has found a satisfactory explanation.

Those who garden according to the moon are not very devout—the only thing that counts is success. Besides, every gardener knows better than all the others, especially as regards the Moon Rules.

Plants that are Ruled by the Moon

In astrology, everything in this world has a special relationship to one of the ten planets. Thus, all plants have their own so-called ruler planet. Knowing which planet rules which plant is especially important for plant healing, which employs plants according to the principles of sympathy or antipathy.

Here you can read which plants the moon influences. The classification is derived from astrological textbooks, not from scientific writing. It is not primarily a question of logic but of imaginative, symbolic thinking. Thus, these classifications are inevitably always subjective.

Do not be surprised if occasionally a plant has a different ruling planet in a different context (e.g., when it is used for a purpose other than healing). Many plants even have several ruling planets. For instance, tomato has Jupiter, Neptune, and Mars. At first glance, few plants have the Moon as their obvious ruling planet, and these do not seem to share common traits. (For example, trees, bushes, flowers, and vegetables that love moisture and/or have white flowers symbolize the humid, watery, bright principle of the moon. These include the following:

- Trees: pear, plum, linden, willow
- Shrubs, bushes: wild rose
- Vegetables: white cabbage, lettuce, cucumber, zucchini, tomato, spinach, mushroom, squash
- Spices: mugwort, vanilla
- Healing plants: blackberry, wild marjoram, marshmallow, lady's mantle, pulsatilla, secale cornutum, American snow ball, dead nettle
- Flowers: daisy, tulip, water lily, violet, miniature wild rose, geranium, iris, Pasqueflower, white rose, honeysuckle
- Fruit: pear, all melons

Moon Rules for Agriculture

No astrologer ever claimed that moonlight influences nature; neither the moonlight, its intensity, or its quantity plays a role in planting. It is the quality of the moonbeams that are important according to astrology.

Llewellyn George

The relationship between plant growth and moon position seems to belong among the oldest and best proven observations. It did not take long for our ancestors to realize the following truism: in addition to plants, the moon influences an entire series of matters in peasant life. Not only do grains and vegetables grow better while the moon waxes, but all of nature is stronger and more immune during a waxing moon, when the life juices are rising. During the waning of the moon the life juices sink.

The Moon Rules derived from these observations were drawn from peasant life but many are valid even in today's agriculture. Perhaps you will find an opportunity to experiment with one of them.

- Turf for fuel must be dug during a waning moon, otherwise it will not burn cleanly and will smoke up the room.
- Slaughter livestock at the full moon; the meat will be juicier and more tender than during a waning moon.
- Animals born during a waxing moon are healthier and more immune than others. Many farmers who know the gestation time of their animals arrange their mating so that the young will be born during a waxing moon.
- All fishermen know that fish bite most at the full moon.
- Even today, wood for carpentry felled during a waning moon, preferably at the new moon, is drier and

more resistant to pests. The wood does not warp or become moldy as easily.

- Theoretically, firewood felled during a waning moon is drier and burns better. In practice, this is a luxury that most lumber companies cannot afford.
- Lumber should not be felled in Cancer or Scorpio because it will be too damp and become moldy too fast.
- Wood for fence posts should be felled during a waning moon, preferably in the fixed signs of Taurus, Leo, and Aquarius, so that it will not get moldy or warp.
- Wean calves during a waxing moon.
- Bread and yeast cake should be baked during the cardinal signs of Aries, Libra, Cancer, and Capricorn. The dough rises higher and the baked goods are fluffier.
- Sheep should be sheared during a waxing moon. The wool will be fuller, thicker, and stronger than during a waning moon.
- Castrate animals during a waning moon. They will bleed less and will get through the ordeal more smoothly.
- Gather oysters during a waxing moon, preferably just before the full moon. They will taste juicier.
- Wash laundry during a waning moon. The dirt will come loose faster.
- Do not make sauerkraut during a Leo moon. It will not draw water.

If the whole course of the world is influenced by the position of the moon, then it must be so for humankind. Understanding this, people began to apply the Moon Rules to their own health and well-being—with obvious success. For many centuries, nobody cared whether science proved the relationship between the moon and earth's phenomena. The important thing was that the rules worked. In modern language, this relationship is called 'the law of lunar sympathy.'

Table 7

Moon Rules for Agriculture

If this table does not specify an individual moon phase or zodiac sign for a certain activity, it is because this does not significantly affect it.

Activity	*Moon*		*Quarter*	*Zodiac sign*
	Waxing	*Waning*		
Baking bread	X		1, 2	Aries, Cancer, Libra, Capricorn
Birthing	X		1, 2	
Brooding eggs of chickens, ducks, and geese	X		1, 2	Cancer, Scorpio, Pisces
Castrating animals		X	3, 4	
Cutting turf for burning		X	3, 4	Aries, Leo, Sagittarius (best)
Felling trees for finish carpentry		X	3, 4	
Fence wood		X	3, 4	Taurus, Leo, Libra
Filling comforters with feathers or wool	X (full moon)		2	
Firewood	X	X	1, 2, 3	

Activity	*Moon*		*Quarter*	*Zodiac sign*
Fishing	X (full moon)		2	
Gathering mussels and oysters	X (full moon)		2	
Hunting	X (full moon)			Libra
Making fences		X	3, 4	Taurus, Leo, Libra
Preparing yeast dough	X		1, 2	Aries, Cancer, Libra, Capricorn
Re-excavating wells	X		1, 2	
Repairing tools				Virgo
Shearing sheep	X		1, 2	
Shoring up wells	X		1, 2	Aquarius
Slaughtering	X (full moon)		1, 2	
Weaning calves	X		1, 2	

Part II

The Influence of the Moon on Health and Beauty

The Moon and Health

I do not know if I understand what you mean by astrology. I do not know all of the influences that go from body to body. I only know when man would not be influenced in some way by a moon or planet, then he would be the only living being wherein this is not the case.

Robert A. Millikan, Nobel Prize Winner and President of California Institute of Technology

Thanks to the discoveries of modern medicine, we live longer than any generation before us. However, humanity's initial euphoria about this progress has since calmed down. It has become clear that, in spite of the progress made by modern medicine and pharmacology, our lives are neither healthier nor happier—merely longer. More and more people are turning to alternative methods in the hope that they will stay healthy as long as possible so that their additional years will be worth living.

The forms of medicine known as 'alternative' generally have their origin in former times or other cultures. Nevertheless, orthodox schools of medicine reject or sneer at them. Of course, one would not expect every treatment to be universally effective simply because people used it in the olden days. For example, Austrians practiced banishment praying (see the following 'Did you know?' box) for centuries. Banishment prayers were used only because nothing else was available. When one's well-being is at stake, a healthy skepticism is good. Healthy skepticism should be applied to alternative medicine as well as to orthodox Western medicine.

The last several thousand years of medical history have not simply brought hocus pocus and charlatanry, as modern medicine would like us to believe. Many treatment methods that were initially regarded as absurd are now given serious consideration by those who previously believed that modern techniques and pharmacology were the last word in medicine.

Sometimes very small things can bring about a change of view. The Chinese have practiced acupuncture for three thousand years with little recognition from Western medicine. Only when the late President Richard M. Nixon became sick during a state visit, and was cured by an acupuncture treatment, was interest sparked among many Western physicians.

Even more interesting medical tidbits have come to us from ancient China. Chinese physicians were expected to prevent illness in their patients. In fact, they could only receive payment if they kept their clients healthy. This was a high standard and, unfortunately, no doctors were able to fulfill it in practice. As a result, three types of physicians developed, differing from one another in rank and prestige. The physicians with the lowest rank were those who treated disease. At the next level were the diagnosticians, especially those who could recognize a disease before it occurred. The highest rank belonged to the physicians whose patients remained free from illness.

If a disease occurred despite all attempts at prevention, the physician in charge could only ask for payment when his patient regained health. In several Chinese provinces, he even had to pay a compensation fee if his patient failed to recover. Worse things happened to the doctor whenever a patient died. The townspeople would hang a special lantern at his office door. If he had too many lanterns, a doctor could be sure that patients would not stand in line at his door.

The Beginnings of Medical Astrology

Although some modern patients may think this old Chinese practice is ideal, any physician would probably be horrified. The truth lies—as always—somewhere in the middle. To put all responsibility on the shoulders of the treating physician is as unfair as to hold the patient himself, or the waxing moon, responsible for healing.

More down to earth than the Chinese model is the method of the Greek physician, Hippocrates, who lived in the fourth century B.C. was the founder of Western medicine. Even today, Hippocrates is regarded as one of the stars of medical history. All physicians must take the famous Hippocratic Oath before they can practice medicine. Only a few, however, understand that the man in whose name they take their professional oath believed in something that most of them consider mumbo jumbo. Hippocrates used astrology as a basis for his medical knowledge. He wrote in his journal: "Only a fool tries to heal without considering the orbits of the planets and stars." Of course, he was not alone in this belief. Paracelsus, Galen, and many other pillars of modern medicine subscribed to the truth of this statement. In fact, healers followed this wisdom for thousands of years as they treated their patients.

Did you know?

Folk Medicine:
A Prescription for Praying Things Away

For centuries, folk medicine employed both healing plants and incantations. Verbal magic, which includes talking, conjuring and praying away a disease, is still practiced in northern Germany. During a waning moon, the healer or wise woman touches the ailing body part and speak a blessing or spell. Many handwritten records indicate that the enchanter's birthday is of the utmost importance for his future career. People born on Christmas Eve, New Year's Day, or during a waxing moon are especially skilled. These moon children allegedly possess the power of 'prayers for shrinking,' allowing them to control the atrophy of living tissue. The following is a typical prayer from Steiermark (a county in Austria) that is used to prevent atrophy. The healer utters this spell over the ailing body part during a waning moon:

Never waste away from flesh and blood.
Legs, marrow, and sinews! Waste not!
God the Father let this grow for now and forever!

The Signs of the Zodiac and Body Parts

In medical astrology, all body parts relate to a sign of the zodiac. The moon is believed to affect the various parts of the body as it transits for two to three days through the corresponding zodiac sign. Treatments for each respective body part work twice as well while the moon is in the appropriate sign. Conversely, anything that afflicts that body part which is also ruled by the sign of the moon's passage, is doubly harmful.

Which Sign of the Zodiac Rules Which Part of the Body?

- *Aries:* head, face (except nose), brain, eyes
- *Taurus:* neck, throat, tonsils, ears, teeth, jaw
- *Gemini:* shoulders, arms, fingers, lungs, thymus gland, upper ribs
- *Cancer:* stomach, diaphragm, chest, lymph system, liver, gall bladder
- *Leo:* heart, aorta, back, spine
- *Virgo:* colon, small intestine, pancreas, nerves, spleen
- *Libra:* kidneys, bladder, inner ear, (sometimes, by association) skin
- *Scorpio:* nose, genitals, rectum, colon, blood, urethra, (sometimes) back
- *Sagittarius:* hip, thighs, liver, veins
- *Capricorn:* teeth, bones, joints, skin
- *Aquarius:* calves, ankles, varicose veins, circulatory system
- *Pisces:* feet, toes, (sometimes by association) lungs, bodily fluids

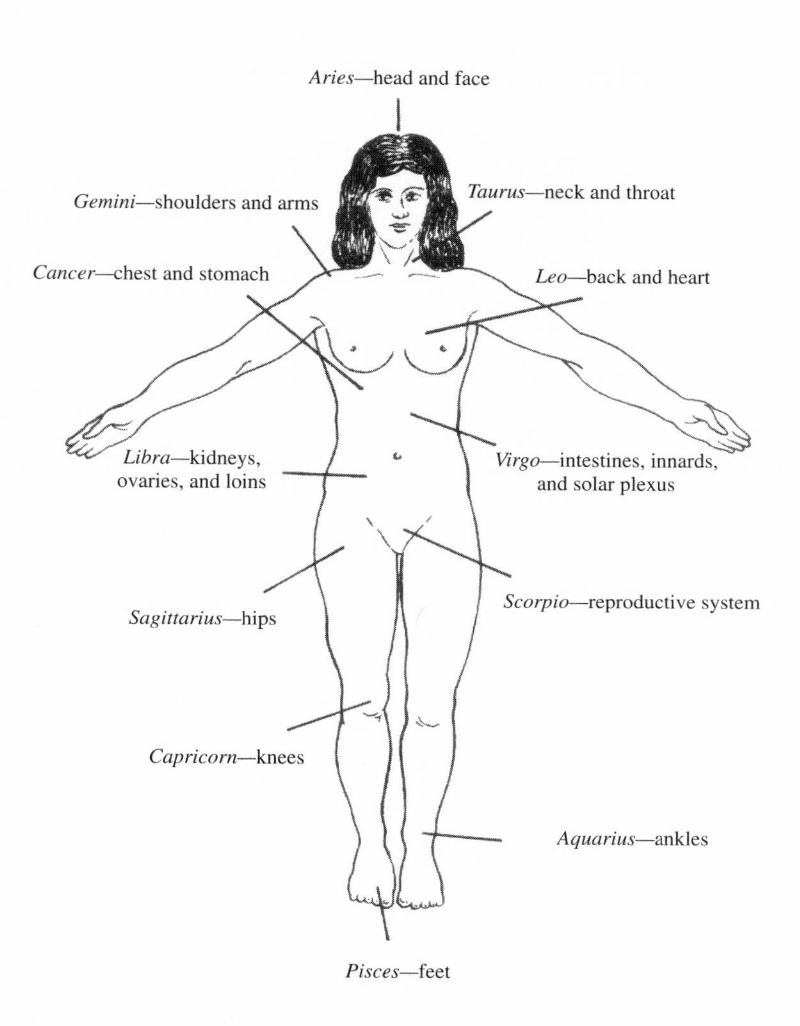

Illustration 6

Classifications According to the Elements

The elements of air, earth, fire, and water rule the individual systems of the body:

- Fire signs (Aries, Leo, Sagittarius) affect primarily the senses
- Earth signs (Capricorn, Virgo, Taurus) affect primarily the circulatory system
- Air signs (Libra, Aquarius, Gemini) affect primarily the glands
- Water signs (Cancer, Scorpio, Pisces) affect primarily the nerves

These relationships have been integral to medical knowledge for thousands of years. Medical astrology involves the diagnosis of illness, or the tendency toward illness, with the aid of the horoscope. A physician who is well-versed in astrology can discern which health problems to expect from a patient's birth chart. If he follows the progressions, he can read if and when a disease will occur, and whether there will be complications. Understanding that the progression of disease corresponds to the lunar phases, he can predict with assurance which days will be critical. On the seventh, fourteenth, twenty-first, and twenty-eighth days after its outbreak, a disease can reach its crisis. The fourteenth day is usually the most dangerous, and is also the date on which more patients die than on any other day. If a patient survives an acute illness until the moon returns to its beginning phase (i.e., the first day of the disease), he is over the hump.

This knowledge was formerly part of the natural healing arts. However, since universities have rejected astrology, medical astrology has become the specialty of sensitive, astrologically talented amateurs. Only a few orthodox physicians are also astrologers. Modern medical schools ridicule the ancient wisdom of the interrelationship of the planets and human health. Interestingly, physicians still repeat the Hippocratic Oath. Would it be too much to ask them to learn a little bit about the man to whom they refer in this vow?

- During a waxing moon, especially at the new moon or the full moon, stimulants are more effective than sedatives. Decrease the dosage of the former and increase the dosage of the latter.
- If the moon conjuncts Saturn, stimulants are less effective. If the moon conjuncts Mars, a healer will be very successful when administering remedies.
- The moon is a life giver as well as a life taker. It carries the life force from the sun down to the earth, and to people. The lunar force can also indicate death.
- At the full moon, floods are higher, bones fill with marrow, oysters are bigger, and fevers are higher.
- During the first half of life, and especially during childhood, the moon predominates. During the second half of life, the sun has a greater influence.
- The moon has a strong influence on lunatics and hysterical, epileptic, and nervous patients. These people feel the influence of the moon very strongly. They are especially restless when the moon is full and should not sleep in direct moonlight.
- During the new moon, the material forces are at their weakest. The waning period between the full moon and the new moon has the strongest spiritual effect because the sun's influence is greatest at that time.
- Never undergo surgery when the moon is in a sign that relates to the body part in question.
- Surgeries performed at the change of the moon are seldom successful. Choose a time when the moon is waxing (i.e., when the moonlight is increasing). Do not perform surgery while the sun is in a sign that rules the body part that will have the incision.
- The moon moves through the entire zodiac in twenty-nine days. Diseases reach a turning point about every seventh day. A change usually occurs after the first week (the first quarter), another one after two weeks

(at the opposition), and another after three weeks. The position of the moon at the beginning of the disease is the starting point for counting the days.

- The moon rules acute illness; the sun rules chronic disease.
- Illnesses that are ruled by the moon are more acute, long, and persistent, but will disappear in twenty-eight days. If the disease is ruled by the sun, then it is more likely to be chronic.
- For surgery, the moon's squares and oppositions to the Sun, Mars, and Saturn should be considered.
- The moon rules a woman's health; the sun influences a man's health.
- When the waxing moon has a positive aspect to the Jupiter in the birth chart, everything that strengthens the heart will succeed. Heart treatments will be successful when the waning moon has a beneficial aspect to Mars, Saturn, and Jupiter. Use heart stimulants with great caution while the moon has negative aspects to the above planets, especially when it is dark or waning.
- Beneficial aspects from the transits of Jupiter or Venus to the moon in the birth chart can be helpful. A square between the moon and sun causes poor vitality. When the progressing moon forms an aspect with the afflicted planet there is cause for concern during an illness. Pay special attention to the transits of the new and full moon.
- Eye ailments may occur if the sun or the moon in the birth chart are positioned in the orbits of the Pleiades (29 degrees in Taurus), Asellus (8 degrees in Leo), or Antares (9 degrees in Sagittarius). This is especially true when Saturn, Mars or Uranus take these places.
- If the moon conjuncts Saturn at the beginning of a disease, it will last a long time.

Did you know?

The Moon and Health at a Glance

- Everything that nourishes the body works better during a waxing moon.
- The waning moon is the best time for surgery, diuretics, diets, detoxification, and everything that needs to be removed from the body.
- Specifically, everything that is good for a body part is especially nourishing when the moon passes through the body part's sign of the zodiac.
- Everything harmful to a body part will affect it strongly while the moon passes through its sign of the zodiac.

The Moon and Disease

All astrologers—and the few astrologer-physicians who still exist—know that people born under a certain moon sign are more prone to certain diseases than are other people. This relationship is derived from the basic principles of astrology. With astrology, one can understand and describe a person's life on all levels simultaneously. In other words, the patient's physical and psychological conditions correspond with one another.

The planets move in regular, exact, and predictable orbits. Thus, it is possible to precisely diagnose the patterns that are activated in a person's life. To do so, physicians trained in astrology must know more than the moon sign. Nevertheless, even knowing only the sun and moon signs can reveal important information about a person's health conditions. On page 119 you can read what to consider if you know your moon sign. In case you do not know what sign your moon was in at the time of your birth, you can calculate the approximate lunar position by using the following tables.

If you want to figure out what sign the moon was in at the time of your birth, begin with Table 8. In the far left column are the years; the other twelve columns show the months.

Find the number at the crossing point between your birth year and your birth month. For example, if you were born in 1963, your

Table 8

Year	January	February	March	April	May	June
1940	12.9	16.5	18.2	21.9	24.6	0.9
1941	23.7	0.0	0.7	4.4	7.1	10.8
1942	6.2	9.9	10.5	14.2	16.9	20.6
1943	16.0	19.7	20.4	24.0	26.7	3.1
1944	25.8	2.2	3.9	7.5	10.2	13.9
1945	9.3	13.0	13.7	17.4	20.0	23.7
1946	19.1	22.8	23.5	27.2	2.5	6.2
1947	1.6	5.3	6.0	9.7	12.4	16.0
1948	11.5	15.1	16.8	20.5	23.2	26.8
1949	22.3	26.0	26.6	3.0	5.7	9.3
1950	4.8	8.5	9.1	12.8	15.5	19.2
1951	14.6	18.3	18.9	22.6	25.3	1.7
1952	24.4	0.8	2.4	6.1	8.8	12.5
1953	7.9	11.6	12.3	15.9	18.6	22.3
1954	17.7	21.4	22.1	25.8	1.1	4.8
1955	0.2	3.9	4.6	8.3	10.9	14.6
1956	10.0	13.7	15.4	19.1	21.8	25.4

number is 9.5. Write the number down and add it to the day of your birth date. If you were born on 17 May, write 9.5 + 17 = 26.5.

With this number, go to Table 9. There, each row has two columns of numbers. The third column lists the zodiac sign. Now, find the column of your personal number. In our example above, 26.5, lies between 25.3 and 27.8. Now you can read, in the column to the right, the moon sign in which you were born. In our example, the birthday 17 May 1963, the moon was in Pisces.

Year	*July*	*August*	*September*	*October*	*November*	*December*
1940	3.6	7.3	11.0	13.6	17.3	20.0
1941	13.4	17.1	20.8	23.5	27.1	2.5
1942	23.3	26.9	3.3	6.0	9.6	12.3
1943	5.8	9.4	13.1	15.8	19.5	22.1
1944	16.6	20.2	23.9	26.6	3.0	5.6
1945	26.4	2.7	6.4	9.1	12.8	15.5
1946	8.9	12.6	16.2	18.9	22.6	25.3
1947	18.7	22.4	26.1	1.4	5.1	7.8
1948	2.2	5.9	9.6	12.2	15.9	18.6
1949	12.0	15.7	19.4	22.1	25.7	1.1
1950	21.8	25.5	1.9	4.6	8.2	10.9
1951	4.3	8.0	11.7	14.4	18.1	20.7
1952	15.2	18.8	22.5	25.2	1.6	4.2
1953	25.0	1.3	5.0	7.7	11.4	14.1
1954	7.5	11.2	14.8	17.5	21.2	23.9
1955	17.3	21.0	24.7	0.0	3.7	6.4
1956	0.8	4.5	8.2	10.8	14.5	17.2

Year	*January*	*February*	*March*	*April*	*May*	*June*
1957	20.9	24.5	25.2	1.6	4.3	7.9
1958	3.4	7.0	7.7	11.4	14.1	17.8
1959	13.2	16.9	17.5	21.2	23.9	0.3
1960	23.0	26.7	1.0	4.7	7.4	11.1
1961	6.5	10.2	10.9	14.5	17.2	20.9
1962	16.3	20.0	20.7	24.4	27.0	3.4
1963	26.1	2.5	3.2	6.9	9.5	13.2
1964	8.6	12.3	14.0	17.7	20.4	24.0
1965	19.5	23.1	23.8	0.2	2.8	6.5
1966	2.0	5.6	6.3	10.0	12.7	16.3
1967	11.8	15.5	16.1	19.8	22.5	26.2
1968	21.6	25.3	27.0	3.3	6.0	9.7
1969	5.1	8.8	9.4	13.1	15.8	19.5
1970	14.9	18.6	19.3	22.9	25.6	2.0
1971	24.7	1.1	1.8	5.4	8.1	11.8
1972	7.2	10.9	12.6	16.3	18.9	22.6
1973	18.0	21.7	22.4	26.1	1.4	5.1
1974	0.5	4.2	4.9	8.6	11.3	14.9
1975	10.4	14.0	14.7	18.4	21.1	24.8
1976	20.2	23.9	25.5	1.9	4.6	8.3
1977	3.7	7.4	8.0	11.7	14.4	18.1
1978	13.5	17.2	17.9	21.5	24.2	0.6

Year	July	August	September	October	November	December
1957	10.6	14.3	18.0	20.7	24.3	27.0
1958	20.4	24.1	0.5	3.1	6.8	9.5
1959	2.9	6.6	10.3	13.0	16.6	19.3
1960	13.8	17.4	21.1	23.8	0.1	2.8
1961	23.6	27.2	3.6	6.3	10.0	12.6
1962	6.1	9.7	13.4	16.1	19.8	22.5
1963	15.9	19.6	23.2	25.9	2.3	5.0
1964	26.7	3.1	6.7	9.4	13.1	15.8
1965	9.2	12.9	16.6	19.2	22.9	25.6
1966	19.0	22.7	26.4	1.7	5.4	8.1
1967	1.5	5.2	8.9	11.6	15.2	17.9
1968	12.3	16.0	19.7	22.4	26.1	1.4
1969	22.2	25.8	2.2	4.9	8.6	11.2
1970	4.7	8.3	12.0	14.7	18.4	21.1
1971	14.5	18.2	21.8	24.5	0.9	3.5
1972	25.3	1.7	5.3	8.0	11.7	14.4
1973	7.8	11.5	15.2	17.8	21.5	24.2
1974	17.6	21.3	25.0	0.3	4.0	6.7
1975	0.1	3.8	7.5	10.1	13.8	16.5
1976	10.9	14.6	18.3	21.0	24.6	0.0
1977	20.8	24.4	0.8	3.5	7.1	9.8
1978	3.3	6.9	10.6	13.3	17.0	19.6

Year	*January*	*February*	*March*	*April*	*May*	*June*
1979	23.3	27.0	0.4	4.0	6.7	10.4
1980	5.8	9.5	11.2	14.9	17.5	21.2
1981	16.6	20.3	21.0	24.7	0.0	3.7
1982	26.5	2.8	3.5	7.2	9.8	13.5
1983	9.0	12.6	13.3	17.0	19.7	23.3
1984	18.8	22.5	24.1	0.5	3.2	6.8
1985	2.3	6.0	6.6	10.3	13.0	16.7
1986	12.1	15.8	16.4	20.1	22.8	26.5
1987	21.9	25.6	26.3	2.6	5.3	9.0
1988	4.4	8.1	9.8	13.4	16.1	19.8
1989	15.2	18.9	19.6	23.3	25.9	2.3
1990	25.0	1.4	2.1	5.8	8.4	21.1
1991	7.5	11.2	11.9	15.6	18.3	21.9
1992	17.4	21.0	22.7	26.4	1.8	5.4

Year	July	August	September	October	November	December
1979	13.1	16.7	20.4	23.1	26.8	2.1
1980	23.9	0.2	3.9	6.6	10.3	13.0
1981	6.4	10.1	13.7	16.4	20.1	23.8
1982	16.2	19.9	23.6	26.2	2.6	5.3
1983	26.0	2.4	6.1	8.7	12.4	15.1
1984	9.5	13.2	16.9	19.6	23.2	25.9
1985	19.3	23.0	26.7	2.1	5.7	8.4
1986	1.8	5.5	9.2	11.9	15.6	18.2
1987	11.7	15.3	19.0	21.7	25.4	0.7
1988	22.5	26.2	2.5	5.2	8.9	11.6
1989	5.0	8.7	12.3	15.0	18.7	21.4
1990	14.8	18.5	22.2	24.8	1.2	3.9
1991	24.6	1.0	4.7	7.3	11.0	13.7
1992	8.1	11.8	15.5	18.1	21.8	24.5

Table 9

from	to	
0.0	2.7	Aries
2.8	5.0	Taurus
5.1	7.3	Gemini
7.4	9.6	Cancer
9.7	11.8	Leo
11.9	14.1	Virgo
14.2	16.4	Libra
16.5	18.7	Scorpio
18.8	20.9	Sagittarius
21.0	23.2	Capricorn
23.3	25.2	Aquarius
25.3	27.8	Pisces
27.9	30.0	Aries
30.1	32.3	Taurus
32.4	34.6	Gemini
34.7	36.9	Cancer
37.0	39.2	Leo
39.3	41.2	Virgo
41.3	43.7	Libra
43.8	46.0	Scorpio
46.1	48.3	Sagittarius
48.4	50.5	Capricorn
50.6	52.8	Aquarius
52.9	55.1	Pisces
55.2	57.4	Aries
57.5	59.8	Taurus
59.9	61.9	Gemini
62.0		Cancer

Comparing verified moon dates from natal charts reveals that this method is fairly correct. Since the moon enters a new sign every two and a half days, more detailed information is beyond the scope of this book. If you want to know the exact position of your moon sign, cast your own horoscope. For this you need your exact time of your birth, which can be obtained at the record office of your birthplace.

The Moon Sign Reveals the Weak Spots in Your Health

Aries

The area typically affected by frequent or chronic disease is the head, eyes, upper jaw, and face, except for the nose. The stormy Aries moon person has to be aware that he is prone to little accidents. Scratches, bruises, and—fortunately usually harmless—burns and cuts are everyday occurrences because he tends to be too impulsive.

Taurus

The problem areas for Taurus moon people are the teeth, ears, neck, throat, and tonsils. There is a tendency toward thyroid disease and sometimes also diabetes. Because of their healthy appetites, people with a moon in Taurus tend to put on more weight than is healthy.

Gemini

The health of Gemini moon people is often very delicate. They are especially vulnerable in the lung area and tend to have asthma, eczema, rheumatism, migraines, psoriasis, and stomach ulcers. Their worst enemies are often their nerves. They need to release so much nervous energy! Sports are especially helpful and sex is another good way to channel the unharnessed energy. Too much carelessness can lead to accidents, with special risk to the arms and legs.

Cancer

Cancer moon people are usually robust and healthy. When they fall ill, they tend to recover quickly. Potential weak areas include the chest, stomach, and gall bladder. Cancer moon people should not fear cancer more than people with other signs. In fact, just the opposite is true: because of their close relationship with their bodies, they become aware of disease before it breaks out, thereby improving their chances for healing.

Leo

The moon is not the only indicator of possible disease. Leo moon people need to be alert to the possibility of latent chronic diseases. They should eat and drink moderately and exercise a lot because their hearts may not withstand a luxurious lifestyle. Spinal problems are also possible, especially during times of psychological stress.

Virgo

People with a moon in Virgo are usually healthy and strong except for their nervous systems. Typical diseases include migraines, allergies, stomach and colonic ulcers, and skin problems. Stress and overwhelming demands have a greater effect on Virgo people than on people of other signs. Relaxation and leisure activities are especially important. Possible serious diseases include anemia, diabetes, appendicitis, and back pain (for tall people).

Libra

Libra moon people are generally robust. However, they tend to have kidney and bladder infections, cyst formation, and skin problems. It is particularly important for them to control their weight and not to smoke.

Scorpio

Scorpio moon people are usually fit and healthy, but tend to be extremely anxious about their health. Weak points are the veins and arteries. Later in life, high blood pressure is also a danger. There is also a tendency to get diseases of the reproductive system and women often suffer from menstruation and heavy menses. Common ailments include headache and migraine.

Sagittarius

Sagittarian moon people tend to eat and drink too much. Thus, they are prone to liver problems. Classic Sagittarian diseases include leg and hip ailments, varicose veins, rheumatism, blood diseases, and (for women) gynecological and menstrual problems.

Capricorn

People with a moon in Capricorn are often healthy and enjoy a long life. They tend to be hard working. Their weak points include the knees, bones, and skin. Rheumatism is a frequent complaint and earaches, nearsightedness, and skin problems are among other common ailments.

Aquarius

People with a moon in Aquarius are usually healthy and strong. Their weak points are the calves and ankles, which can lead to thrombosis and inflammation of the veins. Another, although less serious, problem is the tendency to allergies such as hay fever eczema, asthma, and psoriasis.

Pisces

People with a moon in Pisces often suffer ailments from childhood on. Because of their delicate health, they have long periods of solitude as children. Their energy is also weak as adults, and their nerves are delicate. Common problems for Pisces include heart disease, skin allergies, and asthma. Problems with the feet and lungs can also occur. Smoking is always harmful, but for Pisces moon people it is especially dangerous.

The Sun Sign and Health

Of course, in addition to the position of the moon at the time of birth, the sun also influences health. And because most people know which sign the sun was in at the time of their birth, while only a few know their moon sign, following is a brief summary of typical diseases for each sun sign.

To avoid confusion, I have linked the signs of the zodiac to the four elements.

Sun in a Fire Sign
Aries, Leo, and Sagittarius

People born in one of the three fire signs suffer from diseases that occur suddenly. They may have high fevers and other dramatic symptoms. They recuperate equally quickly. Aries, Leo, and Sagittarius seldom suffer chronic diseases.

Sun in an Earth Sign
Capricorn, Taurus, and Virgo

People born in an earth sign tend to have deeply rooted diseases that manifest after many years, and sometimes become chronic. There is a tendency toward depression. Taurus, Virgo, and Capricorn recuperate from their diseases slowly, but permanently.

Sun in an Air Sign
Libra, Aquarius, Gemini

People born in an air sign tend to psychological and nervous disturbances. Breathing problems, nervous breakdowns, and circulatory disturbances are typical diseases. The likelihood of a complete cure is unpredictable.

Sun in a Water Sign
Cancer, Scorpio, Pisces

People born under a water sign tend to contract strange, difficult to diagnose diseases. There is a tendency toward depression. Whether they are aware of it or note, their recovery depends primarily on their willpower.

Healing Forces Out of Nowhere: That's the Way to Get Rid of Warts

A medical phenomenon that confuses physicians as well as laymen is the placebo effect. A placebo is a drug that does not contain any active ingredient. The healer administers it to give patients the impression that they are receiving some treatment. It can also serve as a control in a double-blind test. In this case, half the patients receive the experimental substance while the other half receive a placebo. Placebos, however, are not always drugs. Many people also believe in the healing effects of copper bracelets, crystals, and rituals. Scientific studies have shown that about 35 percent of all patients who receive placebos feel a noticeable improvement. This is true for both life-threatening diseases and innocuous ailments.

Placebos have been very effective in the treatment of warts. Warts are bumpy formations of the skin caused by a virus. They are ugly, nasty, and occasionally very painful, especially on the soles of the feet. Different cultures have used different rituals for charming warts. Many of these spells correlate with the lunar phases. Most of them, however, are mere superstition. Here are some examples of wart treatments.

- Looking into the full moon, imagine that you are grabbing and throwing the warts behind you (three times).
- Rub your warts with the inside of a banana peel during a waning moon (several times a day).
- Rub the milk of a fig onto your warts during a waning moon.
- Rub your warts with the fresh sap of Celandine (everyday from full moon until new moon).
- At the new moon, rub your warts with dirt. Say, "Luck and blessings, new moon." Then throw the dirt up to the moon.
- During a waning moon, spear black, slimy garden slugs on a stick. Let them die, and your warts will disappear.
- During a waxing moon, stand at a window or go outdoors. Look at the moon and speak while you stroke your warts in the direction of the moon. Say, "May

that which I stroke away become lost. May that on which I look increase."

- Wait until the moon is at least twenty days old. Then lie in a supine position on a path and look at the moon. Rub your wart with whatever you reach out and grab. (This recipe is nearly two-thousand years old, and was written down by Pliny the Elder.)
- Rub your hands under the moonlight.
- Wash your hands under moonbeams in an empty silver bowl (no water).

You might think that these are humbugs and could never work. Surprisingly, each of these methods has worked in many cases; otherwise, they would not have been remembered for centuries. Evidently, in the case of warts, more than for other diseases, faith and the power of the subconscious mind are of great help. Louis Thomas, President Emeritus of the Memorial Sloan-Kettering Cancer Institute in New York, confirms this: "If my subconscious can figure out how the mechanisms necessary to fight the virus work, and how the different cells are able to peel away the tissues, then I can only say that my subconscious is much smarter than I am."

A final wart recipe that I got from a Filipino miracle worker whom I assisted for a few days is as follows: "Cut a little hole in five or six leaves from a birch fig. Put a leaf over each wart so that only the wart peeks through the hole and the rest of the skin is covered. Then burn away the wart with a hot wood coal."

Lino, the healer, assured me that it does not hurt because the leaf poultice protects the skin around the wart. The wart itself is not sensitive to pain. I have not tried this because I can do it in another way, as I mentioned in the preface. Perhaps you do not believe in rituals. However, your dermatologist may have removed warts that later returned. In this case, perhaps you want to try the Filipino healer's method (preferably during a waning moon).

The Moon and Surgery

Socrates left us another important rule that unfortunately has been forgotten over the last few centuries: "Do not let iron touch the part of the body ruled by the present moon sign."

This sounds more mysterious than it is. On page 104 you can see which signs of the zodiac rule which body areas. On these days you should not have surgery on those particular areas of the body. Emergencies, of course, are excluded. The moon spends about two and a half days in one sign. One can look up these days in an ephemeris or (until 1999) at the end of this book. For the forthcoming years it shows the zodiac signs for each days. If you do not follow this advice, according to Hippocrates—as well as many astrologer-physicians—the following problems can arise:

- Complications, such as infections
- Slow, painful healing
- Unexplainable death (e.g., the patient dies after a successful surgery)

If the meaning of Hippocrates' advice is still unclear to you, here are a few practical examples:

- If the moon is in Taurus, you should not have a tonsillectomy.
- Heart surgery is taboo in Leo.
- Surgery on the uterus, ovaries, prostate or other reproductive organs carries a high risk during a Scorpio moon.
- Jaw surgery should not be done in Taurus or Aries.

Linda Goodman is among the renowned astrologers in the United States. She has written many successful books. In *Linda Goodman's Star Signs*, she set out to confirm Hippocrates' theory with a series of examples. Here are a few of her anecdotes.

- The actor Jeff Chandler went into the hospital for a simple disk surgery. He died on the surgery table. The cause of death was unknown. Linda Goodman found out that on the day he died the moon was in Leo, which rules the heart, spine, and back.

- Bertha Todd, the first wife of producer Michael Todd, cut her finger and drove to the hospital for stitches. Afraid of pain, she requested a general anesthetic. Two attempts to sedate her did not work. She never awoke from the third dose. On that day the moon was in Gemini, which rules the shoulders, arms, hands, and fingers.

Ancient wisdom also tells us: "Surgeries performed at the exact point of the moon's changing are seldom successful." In former times, all physicians knew what only a few astrologer-physicians know nowadays. At the change of the moon, wounds bleed more freely than at other times. The Jewish Talmud says that some calendar days (around the full or new moon) are dangerous for bloodletting. (See also "Did you know?" on page 127 " *The Full Moon Is the Best Time to Donate Blood*".) One can only speculate on reasons for this phenomenon. On these days, the body fluids—just as the oceans and all other fluids in nature—are especially responsive to the gravity of the moon. The greatest danger exists at the full moon. Even though most Western physicians regard this theory as nonsensical, scientific research has validated it.

In 1960, the American physician Dr. Edson J. Andrews from Florida investigated tonsillectomies that resulted in complications. These included hemorrhaging cases that were so profuse the patients required remedial care after surgery, as well as cases in which the patients hemorrhaged during surgery, requiring the surgeons to take extreme measures (for such minor surgery) to stop the bleeding. In the sixties, doctors performed tonsillectomies in production lines, which allowed Dr. Andrews to use a large number of cases in his research. In those days, physicians thought that everyone had to get rid of his tonsils at some time, the sooner the better. Subsequently, ear, nose, and throat specialists realized that tonsils are not merely annoying targets for inflammation; they play a very important role in the body.

Dr. Andrews discovered that, in 82 percent of the cases with complications, the operation dates intersected the first quarter and the preceding day of the third quarter. Significant problems occurred around the full moon. Inexplicably, remarkably fewer surgeries were scheduled on new moon days (the second most risky day) than on other days. Andrews compared his data with that of other ear, nose, and throat specialists over a period of six years. He got the same results: the complication rate was highest at the full moon.

Another American colleague, a neurosurgeon, confirmed these observations in neurosurgery. This doctor found that the call for blood transfusions at all the blood banks was highest at the full moon and at the new moon (and up to two days later).

> ***Did you know?***
>
> *The Full Moon Is the Best Time to Donate Blood*
>
> Blood donors should preferably give during a waxing moon—ideally at the full moon, when the body can replace lost blood the fastest.

How Do I Tell My Doctor?

Patients undergoing surgery have many reasons to take seriously the experience of astrologically trained physicians. It would be asking too much for all practitioners of modern medicine to be knowledgeable in astrology. Orthodox medicine could ascertain the truth of Hippocrates' statement with a brief introduction to astrology, a chart, and a glance at an ephemeris. This does not mean that days unsuitable for surgery according Hippocrates should destroy the entire surgical schedule. The moon only stays two and a half days in a single sign, which leaves enough alternate days. On the other hand, if you understand his theory but are afraid of embarrassing yourself in front of your doctor, you could tell a white lie. Unless it is an emergency surgery, you could use a white lie such as: "I have some important things to do at my job; if I do not finish them first, I won't be able to relax after the operation." Most doctors understand such an excuse.

Did you know?

Bloodletting—an Ancient Foolish Practice

Not every folk medicine tradition is correct. Modern medicine recognizes that bloodletting, which is intended to drain bad or excess blood, was a destructive practice. Many patients probably died from it. Today, we can only shake our heads. The only saving factor was that the 'leech' performed his services strictly according to the Moon Rules, usually during a waning moon. Thus, the damage was limited.

In the peasant calendars of the late Middle Ages, bloodletting mannequins demonstrated under which sign one should fight the ailments of certain body parts through bloodletting. A 1766 calendar from the Steiermark says, "Young people a little older than twelve years should bleed after the new moon. Bleed those older than twenty-one after the first quarter, and those older than thirty-six after the full moon. People older than forty-six should bleed after the last quarter. If you have a toothache, bloodletting is good in Sagittarius and Aries moons. Do not leech anyone while the moon is in Leo or Gemini."

Illustration 7: Bloodletting Mannequin, nineteenth century.

Dental Treatment According to the Moon

Just as with surgery, you should also consider the moon for complicated dental treatments. For a relatively simple treatment, such as filling cavities, the position of the moon does not play a very important role—it needs to be done, whether the moon is waning or waxing. However, some Moon Rules state that fillings last longer if the dentist performs them while the waning moon is in a fixed sign (i.e., Taurus, Leo, Scorpio, and Aquarius). Procedures that cause much bleeding, such as periodontal treatments or pulling wisdom teeth should always be performed during a waning moon.

In Kaufbeuren (a Bavarian town), a dentist named Dr. Oscar Hossinger gathered his own statistics over many years of observation. He found that oral healing begins after four days when the surgery has been performed during a waning moon. Healing takes an average of three additional days during a waxing moon. Therefore, he only performs surgery during a waning moon—except, of course, during an emergency.

Dentist Dr. Lieselotte Thrän of Frankfurt recorded the relationship between lunar phases and the cases in her office. Trained in scientific thinking, she admits that she cannot explain certain occurrences. The following phenomena were observed:

- Complications often arise after wisdom tooth surgery performed during a waxing moon.
- Pain occurs more frequently during a waning moon and more patients make emergency appointments because they cannot stand the pain. Such complaints often appear to be emotionally generated. When the patients are in the dentist's chair, the source of their pain cannot be found.
- More appointments are canceled at short notice at the full moon than during any other days of the month.
- During subsequent periodontal treatments, performed within fourteen days, the wound heals remarkably slowly when the moon is in Taurus or Libra, both signs ruled by

Venus. Hardly any complications occur when the moon is in Gemini or Virgo, both signs ruled by Mercury.

By the way: Avoid jaw surgery when the moon is in Taurus!

Weight Loss Diets According to the Moon

If you wish or need to lose weight, then—according to the law of lunar sympathy—the waning moon phase is the best time for flushing and detoxifying the system. Thus, the time of a waning moon offers the best chance to lose excess weight. The best time to start a diet is in one of the three fire signs (Aries, Leo, and Sagittarius). Then, the excessive fat in your body can (hopefully) burn away!

Which dieting technique you select is up to you. How many pounds do you want to lose? How long should your diet last? What foods can you most easily avoid and what are irresistible? In addition, your approach to weight loss depends on your moon sign. Dr. Klaus Meyer, a Munich physician who specializes in natural healing and medical astrology, says, "It is nearly impossible to persuade a Taurus moon person to go on a diet; he loves to eat. A Scorpio moon person would never start a thousand-calorie diet; whenever he feels overweight, he practically fasts until he has resumed his desired weight. Libra moon people never need to lose weight; they are far too concerned about their appearance and make certain they never gain a single extra pound."

These days, it is unusual that someone wants to gain weight. Nevertheless, if you want to gain a few pounds, you have to start the anti-diet during a waxing moon. Preferably the moon should be in a water sign (Cancer, Scorpio, and Pisces), when your appetite is greater and your body is more ready to store the additional food.

Renouncing Favorite but Unhealthy Habits

If you want to stop drinking or smoking, any effort in that direction is helpful. Start during a waning moon in an infertile sign—remember the fertile and infertile signs listed in the gardening section? The ideal signs are Gemini, Leo, and Virgo. The worst of the ordeal may already be behind you when you reach the more difficult days of the waxing moon.

Did you know?

The Spa Has Its Origins in the May Bath

The cure that is designed to restore the life force has its roots in an ancient tradition: the May Bath. Our ancestors were in the habit of going to a spa with healing waters in May because it was commonly believed that one's life force needed to be reawakened after a long winter of deprivation.

People could enjoy the blossoming of nature—but not only nature; apparently the spa romance already existed in those days! Ancient writings speak of experienced spa girls who collected herbs and steeped them in huge vats of hot, healing waters. No one has divulged in detail what else they did to make their customers happy. Since the fourteenth century, the ecclesiastic circles protested such high-spirited behavior in the spas. However, all tirades and restrictions were of little effect.

Anyone who could afford it went to the spa during May. The month of May was nearly a must from the medical point of view, and for good reason. In those days, the lunar year began in the spring, and consisted of thirteen lunar months. Each lunar month was twenty-eight days long. A person would work for twelve months, after which he needed to rejuvenate.

If not, the thirteenth month would bring misfortune. The tired body would be so susceptible it could not resist disease. Spring fatigue and other ailments would result. For this reason, people dedicated the thirteenth month to health. The life force was reawakened in May. Only then could one hope to stay strong enough to survive the next twelve-month cycle.

The Moon and Fertility

Although our ancestors may have been as naive, at least in some areas, as we tend to believe they were, when it came to sexuality and fertility, they did not experiment the way people—who allegedly know the facts of life—do in our modern society. In a culture in which fertility was important for survival, the relationship between menstruation and birth was everyday knowledge. Furthermore, it was universally understood that the moon played an important role.

Our ancestors were as ignorant as we are today about the nature of that role. Nevertheless, there was a fundamental difference. Ancient speculation was of a much more delightful and human character than that offered by modern moon researchers. The idea of the man in the moon haunted many ancient cultures. He stepped down to earth on full moon nights and made sleeping girls pregnant with a moonbeam. This explanation appears in so many different cultures that one might assume it was really believed, not just used as an excuse!

Archeologists discovered a few years ago how well-informed historical peoples were about the acts of procreation and birth. They discovered prehistoric (originating from 30,000 B.C.) menstruation calendars carved in bone and ivory. These calendars marked all the important dates, including fertile days (around the full moon) and the number of lunar months until the expected birth.

Much more recently—but nevertheless 5,000 years ago—fertility peg calendars, dedicated to the moon goddess Astarte, were used. These little clay figurines had twenty-nine to thirty holes, symbolizing the number of days in the synodic moon orbit and the time between two menstruation cycles. No doubt, our ancestors were knowledgeable.

The moon and its phases became the symbol for the eternal circle of procreation: birth (the small sickle at the horizon), growth (waxing to full moon), ailing and dying (waning moon), death (the three moonless nights of the new moon), and rebirth (the reappearance of the moon sickle after the moonless nights). According to our ancestors, the planets were gods. The deity responsible for fertility was, of course, the moon goddess. The most powerful figure of all, she was the ruler of the life-giving waters—streams as well as oceans—and the archetype of femininity. More than all the other gods, she captured humanity's veneration. People from cultures all over the world have worshipped this great goddess for thousands of years in different ways. In her bright phase, she is seen as giving life and fertility; in her dark phase, she symbolizes the destructive forces of nature in the eternal cycle of death and rebirth.

The fertility rules from ancient times can easily be applied to modern times. They can even be useful when one is not familiar with mythology. Still, the myths associated with the moon goddess are so beautiful that everyone who does not know about them is missing something. Here you can read about Inanna and Diana, Demeter and Artemis, Hecate and Persephone. You can also read about their relationship to fertility, the explanation for this, and what was valid in those days that is still valid today.

Did you know?

All These Things Symbolize the Moon

In astrology, the moon stands for:
sensitivity, pregnancy, emotions, feelings, mother, pool, perceptivity, peasants, ocean, the unconscious mind, menstruation, sucking, capriciousness, childhood, nourishment, passivity, pleasure, stomach, receptivity, water, weak-mindedness

The Moon Goddess—the Symbol of Fertility

The sun god and the moon goddess have enjoyed adoration throughout the world. They appear in the myths of all cultures and often have very similar legends. Sometimes they even swap genders, so that there is a sun goddess and a moon god. However, the moon deity has been feminine for thousands of years in all the great civilizations. These cultures worshipped both the sun and moon as opposing forces of the same principle. The sun generates warmth, light, and creative energy. The moon is the force from which new life derives, and brings humidity and fertility to humans, animals, and plants. However, it is both sun and moon together that create the necessary conditions for life.

In the ancient religions, the moon goddess was of a higher rank. At the time of the full moon, festivals were held in her honor. *The Mists of Avalon* by Marion Zimmer Bradley has brought many people back to celebrating Beltana, or May Day. The first full moon after the spring equinox marks the beginning of spring, which is a time of solemn festivities. Festive ceremonies—as well as highly non-ceremonial fertility activities—occurred at the time of the harvest moon in the autumn. According to the records of Ovid and other chronologists, morals and scruples were not upheld at such times because of the popular belief that wild activities during the harvest festival had a direct affect on the fields' fertility in the New Year. Ovid says that, when the orgy participants staggered home in the early morning hours, passersby greeted them with respect and called them blessed because they had appropriately honored the moon goddess. American author Paul Katzeff mentioned this episode in his book *Moon Madness*, adding with regret, "Today at such occasions, men have to be content with a platonic ride on the hay wagon."

Around three thousand B.C., the downfall of ancient religion began, as the matriarchs of these ancient civilizations gave way to patriarchs. Likewise, moon goddesses gave way to sun gods, until finally—in Christianity, as well—the goddesses were relegated completely to the realm of darkness and magic. The dark (new moon), however, is only one aspect of the moon cycle and the feminine archetype that it reflects is not at all negative. Early peoples knew that the force of new life derived from the dark phases of the moon. However, throughout thousands of years, this was forgotten and people began to fear the dark moon. Supported by the patriarchs, this attitude continued for centuries and it still exists today.

Plutarch wrote the words that became the credo for the next two thousand years, which is still in the minds of people today: "The waxing moon is full of good intentions, but the waning moon brings disease and death."

Although many civilizations have attempted to do so, it is nearly impossible to describe the many qualities of one moon principle in a single deity. (For instance, the Sumerians had only Inanna.) Elizabeth Hämmerling has described in her book *Moon Goddess Inanna* how the myth of the heavenly goddess corresponds with the lunar phases. However, most civilizations had more than one moon goddess, at least one for each lunar phase. The great goddess had many names, for example:

In the Middle East: *Inanna, Tiamat, Ishtar, Astarte*
In Ancient Egypt: *Isis, Hathor, Neith, Maat*
In Ancient Rome: *Juno, Diana, Luna, Titania*
In Greece: *Demeter, Hera, Artemis, Aphrodite, Selene, Persephone, Hecate, Europa, Pallas Athena*
In India: *Shakti, Aditi, Durga*
In Tibet: *Tara*
In China: *Quan Yin*
In Japan: *Kannon*

Later, she appeared as Mary in Christianity. In many old pictures, the Madonna stands on a moon sickle. Initially, the new religion was without a feminine deity. However, in areas where the old religions were still known, Christianity could only attract followers by incorporating adoration of the Virgin Mary. Thus, at least indirectly, the cult of the virgin goddess Artemis-Diana continued.

Many of the moon goddesses, each representing a phase of the moon, are familiar to us through myths. In our civilization, the Greek goddesses and gods are the best known.

Artemis (the Roman Diana) represented the new moon (first quarter). The courageous young ruler of wild animals, she was also the goddess of the legendary Amazons. She was a classic moon lady and a symbol of the first of the four moon quarters (new moon to half moon). The goddess of the hunt mostly dwelled in nature and her unsteady hunting life symbolized the principle of the mutable. She was completely celibate, but was nevertheless protective of midwives and women in childbirth. She expressed the double character of the moon principle: she was both the goddess of the hunt and the protector of animals. With her death arrows she could kill anybody and she could also heal all those who suffered. Men and women prayed to her for fertility, successful childbirth, and good luck in hunting.

Demeter, the goddess of the wheat fields, the symbol of fertility, and the motherhood principle, represented the second quarter (waxing to full moon). In her happiness, she blessed the earth so that harvest time would never end and there would never again be wintertime or hunger. The joyful young goddess Demeter, whose priestesses taught men and women the secrets of marriage, had a daughter (Persephone) by her brother, Zeus. She usually appeared with Persephone, who was also called Kore. After Persephone grew up, the ruler of the underworld (Hades or Pluto) fell in love with her. He kidnapped her and took her to the realm of death. In her sorrow, Demeter forbade the trees to bear fruit and the plants to grow so that humanity faced extinction if her daughter was not returned. In despair, Demeter searched for nine days and nights and finally found Persephone with the help of Helios and Hecate. Persephone had meanwhile become a mother herself. At the happy reunion, she held Pluto's child in her arms. Zeus struck a compromise: for one half of the year, Persephone would rule the underworld; in the other half, she would live in the light with her mother.

Selene, the moon goddess personified, represented the full moon. She often appeared with wings and a moon crown, sitting in a moon wagon drawn by two white horses. According to mythology, she disappeared into the marriage bed of the sun god during the time of the new moon. Thus, the sky stayed dark. In classic mythology, her love for Endymion, a shepherd of unimaginable beauty, immortalized her. One night, as he slept by his flock in the mountains, Selene, who was rising in the sky, saw him. Immediately, she fell in love with him. She stepped down from the sky, and lay down with him. In a jealous moment, she decided that no one else should enjoy his beauty, so she gave him the kiss of eternal sleep. Night after night, she visited him and covered him with kisses. However, her love did not bring her good fortune because her beloved never awoke.

Persephone and Hecate symbolized the third and fourth quarter (waning to full moon). Persephone, the daughter of Demeter, depicted the more pleasant story. Because she had to stay half of the year in the realm of death as the wife of Pluto, the god of the underworld, she welcomed the souls of the diseased and accompanied them lovingly to Hades. Through her life in two worlds, Persephone symbolized the transition of death to rebirth, and the principle of hope.

In Greek mythology, Hecate, the horrible goddess of the night, personified the dark moon (the three new moon nights) in its blackest and most hopeless form. She appeared in her wagon, drawn across the night sky by black horses, together with her horrible daughters, who were responsible for nightmares and madness. She seduced men, sucked their blood, and ate their flesh. Hecate was the goddess of magic, the highest witch priestess, and the guardian at the threshold of death. Throughout history, she evolved into a symbol of evil:

Greece: *Medusa, Medea, Circe*
India: *Kali*
Hebrew: *Lilith*
Sumeria: *Ereshkigal*
Britain: *Morgana*
Scandinavia: *Hel*
Germany: *Frau Holle, the evil fairy, the evil witch*

These corrupt ladies and their black magic were depicted in art using the symbols of the dark moon (a black circle), the reversed moon (horns), and a flat bowl turned upside down so that all blessings pour out. Even today, we view the fourth moon phase in this negative manner.

When the sun gods Gilgamesh, Amun Ra, Zeus, Yahweh, and Apollo replaced the great goddesses Inanna, Ishtar, Isis, Demeter, Artemis, and Persephone, civilization forgot the teachings of the goddess. The only one among the great goddesses who remained, was Hecate. The downfall of the old religion has been linked to the Inquisition, when wise women fell to the hand of religious persecution and burning. The defamation of womankind continued for many centuries.

Now, the new era of the Aquarian Age is dawning. Slowly, once again, we have begun to view the dark side of the moon as a requirement for something new to spring forth. Femininity is no longer associated with misuse, evil, black magic, forbidden sex, the occult, violence, and death. Slowly, Hecate is becoming Artemis again. Out of the darkness, new life is beginning to grow.

> ***Did you know?***
>
> *Love According to the Moon*
>
> I heard the following story in Zimbabwe, a state in Southern Africa.
> In ancient times, the people of Zimbabwe chose a new king every year. During festival ceremonies, they sacrificed the old one for the sake of his tribe. There was no questioning; it was destiny. Before the sacrifice, the king married, because the village expected him to father a son. Royal blood was in short supply, due to the short length of each reign; thus, the king's counselors did not ask any questions concerning succession. They choose the date of the wedding and the few mating nights strictly according to the lunar phases. The most important time for love was around the full moon.

The Moon and Menstruation

Our word 'menstruation' is derived from the Latin word for month, *menses*. A lunar month spans two full moon phases, which is exactly 29.5 days. This is the period between two average menstruation cycles. Nowadays, we speak about the rhythm of a twenty-eight day cycle. However, recent studies show that the average period is actually between twenty-nine and thirty days.

The relationship between the moon and menstruation was very clear to our ancestors. Aristotle explained that the moon stimulated the endometrial lining, increasing it a little more every day and filling it with nutrients to prepare it for the day new life would start to grow in it. Such a weighty explanation passed over the heads of his contemporaries. The more popular theory was that the moon goddess had a menstruation cycle. She had her period only during the new moon, when she would withdraw for a few nights. On earth, women followed her example.

Modern scientists believe that, in ancient days, most women of the same tribe menstruated at the same time, at the new moon. In some cases, this is still valid. Biologists have observed that women in the same family or household or commune (who live in close contact with each other) tend to have "synchronistic menstruation cycles," as they say with typical scientific caution. The probable explanation is that pheromones stimulate the body to release hormones that lead to expelling of an unfertilized egg. The synchronicity of cycles had interesting consequences in ancient times. When the majority of women menstruated at the new moon, their fertile days were at the full moon phase. According to nature, women enjoyed love most on their fertile days. The future of the population often rested on what occurred during full moon nights. The results of these hot nights manifested exactly nine (synodic) lunar months later, when—logically, again at full moon—a large number of babies entered the world.

More Births at the Full Moon?

In our time, however, this trend is no longer so clear. Changing influences in the environment, ranging from birth control pills to isolated living situations, have caused many women's cycles to lose their natural closeness to the moon. Thanks to the Pill, women can choose menstruation times to accommodate their schedules. Nevertheless, even nowadays, many midwives and birth clinicians claim that maternity wards are especially active on full moon nights. Many scientists and statisticians, however, would strongly contradict this claim.

Due dates are a classic topic for research, leading to countless studies and tall piles of dissertations. Walter and Abraham Menaker are American birth clinicians who checked the birth statistics for many years in all the hospitals of New York City. They proved that, among millions of births, most occurred on the three days around the full moon. On the other hand, scientists of the opposing camp, who tried with expensive research projects to prove the contrary, were also successful. Among these scientific studies, which only involved a smaller number of cases, a series of unpredictable factors (e.g., induced birth or Cesareans) significantly influenced the results. For this reason, a firm conclusion regarding this subject will not be forthcoming soon. One thing, however, is certain: the synchronism that existed in the olden days between the lunar phases and fertility is no longer obvious.

The Czech physician Dr. Eugen Jonas, who became famous in the sixties, claims that even today each woman has a unique and clear cosmo-biological relationship. She can use this as insurance, either to become pregnant or to avoid pregnancy. Although Dr. Jonas' method became well-known, his enemies in the orthodox scientific field were equally vocal. They criticized him for selling his fertility calendar at the extravagant price of more than two to three hundred dollars. This calendar—named after Jonas—enabled every woman to monitor her fertile and non-fertile days for one year. Nevertheless, his theory has convinced many women—and even some orthodox physicians—to follow it. The following is a brief introduction to his cosmo-biological method for birth control.

Family Planning According to the Moon

Dr. Jonas remembered the teachings of ancient Egypt, Greece, and Babylon, where physicians were also astrologers. According to Hippocrates, "A physician ignorant of astrology does not have the right to call himself a physician."

For many years, Jonas studied the relationship between astrology, astronomy, and gynecology. Finally, he made a sensational discovery. In addition to the well-known ovulation cycle, each woman has a second unique fertility cycle that depends on the moon phase at the time of her birth. This is valid for her entire life. Ovulation cycles and moon cycles may have been synchronized during ancient times. However, through the inventions of modern life (e.g., electric light, the Pill, and the small family), this rhythm was disrupted. According to Dr. Jonas, the phase of greatest sexual excitation is still valid, but the ovulation of modern women is no longer synchronized with the moon, only with her individual moon phase. In other words, most women do not have a single fertility cycle, but two. One depends on ovulation, the other on the individual moon phase, the position of the moon at the time of her birth.

After much research, Dr. Jonas found that 85 percent of successful fertilizations happened within the moon cycle, and only 15 percent within the ovulation cycle. This could explain why some fertile couples cannot get pregnant despite love making precisely according to the biological calendar. This also explains why pregnancies can occur during menstruation, which is nearly impossible under the laws of Western medicine. According to Jonas, fertility is highest when both cycles are synchronized, as was usual in the ancient days. He developed a method to exactly calculate the fertile moon phase days. These dates can be used to prevent conception or to invite it with a greater chance of success. In the Jonas Fertilization Calendar, a woman can look up the moon phase at the time of her birth and the expected dates of ovulation. With these dates, she can either calculate the optimal time to conceive or to (with the right means) prevent pregnancy.

Did you know?

Pregnancy—Nine or Ten Moon Months?

The moon is still the reference for calculating the duration of a pregnancy. Nine months means exactly nine synodic months, which equals 265.5 days. The number nine, by the way, is the number of the Greek moon goddess.

Finally, Dr. Jonas succeeded in precisely predicting the date a woman who used his calendar should choose if she wanted to conceive a son or a daughter. His statistical success rate was an unbelievable 98 percent. He simply determined the days that, according to the laws of classical astrology, were in a masculine or a feminine moon sign. For instance, only sons were conceived on Leo days, while Virgo days produced only daughters.

The entire school of medicine ran amok when they heard this thesis. However, Jonas passed—with glory—all the challenges of the enraged scientific establishment. A committee of gynecologists presented him with the conception dates of babies who were about to be born. Dr. Jonas had to consider the information and then predict the gender of each child. His colleagues were astounded when he correctly predicted 87 percent of the cases—and this even when some of the data undoubtedly included errors. Later studies of women who conceived their much-wanted children according to his calendar showed a 98 percent success rate.

Similarly accurate (i.e., 97 to 100 percent) is Jonas' cosmobiological method for preventing pregnancy. His followers maintain that this method provides a certainty factor equal to that provided by birth control pills, which are 98 percent effective. His enemies think he is a lunatic; his followers, including orthodox physicians, think him a wise man. Which is true, you will have to decide for yourself.

If you want to test this method, you only have to pay one tenth the former fee. Just consult the book *Cosmo-biological Birth Control* by Shalila Sharamon and Bodo J. Baginski, which features a Jonas fertility calendar that has been calculated by computer specialists based on ephemerides. An ephemeris is a table of the star positions, calculated many years in advance by mathematicians and containing the precise positions of the planets for every day of the year. According to the fertility calendar, you can find out the moon position at the time of your birth, as well as fertile and infertile days for family planning. I can't guarantee anything, but I wish you luck.

Did you know?

Folk Medicine—A Girdle for the Moon Goddess

In the Middle Ages, an important medical technique was the so-called girdling of the pregnant woman's belly, symbolizing protection from all danger. People in southeastern Europe still practice this custom, which was already considered ancient during the Middle Ages. In the olden days, pregnant women wore girdles made of deer hide, linen, or hemp. The girdle was removed just before delivery to facilitate birth. The ceremonial loosening of the girdle before delivery was a favored medical treatment during Greek and Roman times. After a successful birth, the mother consecrated her girdle to the generous goddess Diana, protector of expectant mothers, thereby thanking her for helping during childbirth.

The Moon and Madness

Did you know?

Johannes Kepler's Old Whore:
"The moon alone gives me more trouble than all planets put together."

Johannes Kepler proved that the earth and planets revolve around the sun. He dealt the final death blow to Ptolemy's geocentric system. He fought passionately against the "old whore astrology." Nevertheless, he never could leave her alone. The above quote is an extraction from a letter dated 1601. In it, Kepler declared that he felt sick and uncomfortable with himself. At the same time he offered the above explanation for his feelings.

As anybody knows, a lot goes on during full moon nights. Hospital psychiatric wards are full of unstable people who get especially wound up. Epileptics suffer stronger attacks than on other days of the month, unless they have taken enough preventive medication. Depression and suicide calls pile up on telephone hotlines. Fire stations are on alert, as are police stations and emergency rooms. There are more sleep walkers on the roofs. It has always been this way. Everyone who deals with these cases knows that the full moon brings crises to a head.

Only modern scientists still resist this connection. They do not approve of the methods from which these statistics were derived. Our ancestors, however, did not have a problem with this correlation. For them, the full moon had an undeniable relationship with madness, including all the variations of abnormal behavior. One only has to look around in order to see the truth of this. If people periodically have a fit, the moon is usually involved. In ancient times, people had already made a connection between epileptic attacks and the moon. These attacks increased with the waxing moon and reached their peak at full moon.

The famous physician Galen believed that women with menstruation problems had a special disposition to epilepsy. He believed that the disease was halted when the menses returned to its regular pattern. He suggested that his patients wear a mandrake root around their necks. Healers considered mandrake a highly potent remedy against epilepsy and disturbances in fertility. (More about this is in "Magic Herbs" on page 237 and 240.)

Such relatively scientific explanations, however, were more the exception than the norm. Many ancient authors wrote nonsensical explanations about the interrelation between the moon and behavior. Hippocrates assumed that visits of the moon goddess caused nightmares and sleepwalking. Plutarch warned that anyone stupid enough to sleep in the moonlight would surely lose his mind. The Jewish Talmud also warned people against sleeping in moonlight, as did the New Testament. Paracelsus wrote that the moon's gravitational force causes madness; he said that, just as the North Pole pulls the arrow of a compass, gravity pulls the clear thinking out of a person. In her book *Causae et Curae* (Causes and Cures), Hildegard von Bingen wrote the dark prognosis that boys conceived a few days after the full moon would be insane. Even more risky would be to conceive a son on the fourth day after the full moon: "He will always be a thief, and long for things that belong to others."

The mind-damaging effects of the full moon have been expressed in the literature of folk medicine over many centuries, as well as in peasant customs. Austrian professor Herman Wohlgenannt collected a series of examples in his book *The Moon*:

- The marriage bed should be protected from moonlight.
- Conception in the moonlight results in crazy and sleepwalking children.
- Pregnant women should not look into the moonlight

or be struck by moonbeams, or their children will be born as lunatics.

- If a man passes water and then makes love to his wife, she will become 'moon pregnant' and give birth to a baby that is deformed, severely retarded or—at best—slow.

Another association is between the full moon and death:

- Do not leave children's laundry outside in the moonlight. One who dries laundry in the moonlight dries "death laundry."
- Whoever sews in the moonlight is sewing his shroud.
- One should not spin yarn in the moonlight; the yarn will come apart and will become the shroud of the spinner's child.

In sixteenth century Europe, hardly anybody dared to walk the streets at the full moon. Everyone was afraid of werewolves. The werewolf legend was already ancient at that time. Many cultures have countless old and new horror stories that vary in detail, but agree on one point: a human can transform into a wild beast at the full moon. With so many scary stories, it is no wonder that even today many people draw their curtains tight against the full moon—not just to keep the brightness out of their bedrooms.

Strong evidence has strengthened superstitions about the dangerous effects of the full moon. American journalist Collie Small discovered that the crucifixion occurred during a full moon. The Roman senate assassinated Julius Caesar at the full moon. The assassinations of Alexander Trotsky, Austrian chancellor Dollfuß, and the Russian Czar Alexander II, as well as the My Lai massacre in Vietnam all took place at the full moon. Most of Jack the Ripper's wrongdoings and, more recently, five or eight of New York serial killer Son of Sam's murders took place at the full moon. Until the beginning of the nineteenth century, caretakers in British mad houses (e.g., London's Bethlehem hospital) would beat their patients just before the full moon. The doctors prescribed this as a preventive measure, but it did not keep the pa-

Illustration 8
Han Weiditz, 1517.
A Witch, Transformed into a Werewolf, Attacks a Traveler.

tients from becoming violent during the full moon.

Science, however, has never really addressed this subject. American psychiatrist Dr. Arnold Lieber is an exception. In the seventies, he reviewed the few existing studies about the influences of the moon, conducted his own research, and published a book on the subject, *The Lunar Effect*. Those scientific studies that examine the relationship between the moon and violence, madness, arson, suicide, and similar emotional aberrations verify, in essence, everything the nonscientific world has always known. By the way, Dr. Lieber was staunchly against astrology, which he ridiculed as "cosmic pseudo-science." However, his explanations for moon-dependent phenomena would satisfy any astrologer. He suggested the theory that the right, intuitive half of the brain was the moon half, and the left, logical side of the brain was the sun half. He explained the increasing rate of crime and violence as a result of modern people's increasing suppression of the moon half. The escalating effects seen at the full moon are a result of this repression.

This research led to a revolt in the scientific world, which was highly indignant that the moon—which brings no more light into a room than a small candle—should possess such power over humanity. All of a sudden, many studies were undertaken to contradict Dr. Lieber's results, or to blame him for shoddy scientific work. Perhaps because they could not explain the phenomenon, busy scientists worked for months to prove that the moon's correlation to violence, madness, and other deviations was a mere coincidence. As of today, the jury is still out with respect to who is correct.

Now we turn to the latest proof in a related—although much more harmless—subject.

Sleepwalkers and Lunatics

"TOMORROW IS THE FULL MOON—70,000 PEOPLE WILL SLEEPWALK IN MUNICH." Thus read the headline of a major Munich street paper, dated 6 February 1993. It continues:

Mystic moon: some can't fall asleep, while others sleepwalk through the area. One child out of ten and six adults out of a hundred are on their way during sleep—especially at the full moon. It drives them out of bed. Science does not have any proof for the moon-man relationship. Sleep researchers and psychologists can only guess at or assume the powerful influence of this heavenly body. Those who feel its influence declare: "I am a lunatic." Everyone has a story about the full moon. However, it is still a puzzle for science. This earth satellite influences the tides and some animals love and live according to the moon phases. Its influence on human beings cannot be proven. One explanation for sleepwalking at the full moon is the light theory. The brighter the light is, the more restless the sleeper becomes. Sleepwalkers usually move to a light source. We do not know the reason for this.

"However, it is very rare for the moon to shine into a room," Munich psychologist Dr. Paul Kochenstein admits. "Nevertheless, the subconscious mind does play an important role. Man always looks for an explanation for what he is doing. In the case of sleepwalking, if he thinks the full moon is responsible for sleep-

walking, then he suggests just that to himself, and I guarantee that he will be on his way the next time he falls asleep during a full moon."

In other words, science still cannot explain seventy-thousand Munich people sleepwalking during the full moon. Still, it does know what one should not do to a sleepwalker: this is, one should not awaken him. *When someone snaps out of a sound sleep, he is startled. It is better to direct them gently back to bed.* For thousands of years, people have been doing this naturally with the sleepwalking members of their tribes and families.

Did you know?

The Moon and Madness Are Related to One Another by Language

Many languages still show a clear relationship between the moon, the Latin word for which is Luna (the Moon goddess), and madness:

- English—lunacy (madness)
- Italian—lunatico (mad)
- French—avoir des lunes (to be crazy)

In eighteenth century England, the judicial system clearly defined the legal difference between a lunatic (who only goes mad once a month) and an insane madman (who is always and hopelessly mad).

Herbal Medicine and the Moon

Since ancient times, plants have had an important place in folk medicine. A collection of medicinal plants was buried in the grave of a Neanderthal man, who died about 60,000 years ago. An unknown Sumerian wrote the first herb book 5,000 years ago. The title "Father of the Art of Herb Healing" belongs to the Greek physician Pedanios Dioskurides, who lived in the first century after Christ. His work *De Materia Medica* listed six hundred plants and their medicinal effects. This work, along with the *Natural History* by Pliny the Elder (who died in 79 A.D.) became the pharmacological standard for the following fifteen hundred years. Except for a few minerals and word charms, there were no other types of remedies until the beginning of the present era. Middle European herbalists tried to discover counterparts for the Mediterranean herbs in the unfavorable climate of their own region.

People copied and annotated the old herb books over and over again; however, not all scribes made correct copies of the original texts by Pliny and Dioskurides. Hildegard von Bingen, a German Abbess of the twelfth century, was an herbalist, clairvoyant, healer, and prophetess. Her writings *Physica* and *Causae et Curae,* mentioned the Latin names and the common German names for many plants, which helped to diminish the source of mistakes.

Paracelsus von Hohenheim (1493-1541) was the medical Luther of the sixteenth century. He was the greatest physician of his time because of his powerful intuition. He is considered the forerunner of homeopathy because he declared that what makes a person sick can also heal him. He not only claimed this theory, but apparently also proved it. When the plague erupted while he was in Sterzing (in southern Tyrol), he allegedly healed many people by giving them minuscule doses of their own excrement in a bread pill. Paracelsus reputedly gained his knowledge not only from his university studies, but also by learning about the effects of healing plants from the gypsies. He traveled with them throughout Europe for many years to learn their healing arts. Nevertheless, he was still fallible. He claimed that the outer recognizable feature of a plant indicated its use as a remedy. The walnut, for example, which reminds one of a brain, he said was a good remedy for headache. He used hairy roots as a remedy for baldness. According to modern medicine, of course, this is nonsense. Yet, this superstition remained for hundreds of years.

Even at the beginning of the present century, half of physicians' prescriptions were derived from the old herb books. English herbalist Nicholas Culpeper's (1616-1654) book *Complete Herbal* was the bible of herb healing for centuries. Even today it is recommended reading for all medical students. Culpeper insulted the English faculty by translating their Latin pharmacology into English. He became famous in astrological medicine because he listed the ruling planet for each plant. Many astrologers, however, consider his classifications arbitrary.

Collecting Healing Plants

Often, a plant has a very magical use for healing. All ancient books on folk medicine tell when and under which conditions to gather healing plants and herbs. Certain beliefs were held with respect to herb gathering:

- Only pick plants at the right time and in the prescribed way to develop their full effect.
- Collect plants silently before sunrise. Nobody should speak to the gatherer.
- Certain times and special days are especially favorable, such as Maundy Thursday, Good Friday, May Day, Ascension Day, and St. John's Day (24 June), Midsummer's Night, and Mary's Assumption (15 August).
- The moon phases are also very important.
- Plants whose roots or wood are to be used should only be gathered during a waning moon, ideally at the new moon.

- Plants whose flowers or blossom hips are used were collected by the wise old-time herbalists only during a waxing moon.
- At the full moon, plants contain the most active agents.
- Sometimes a great part of the effect depends on the magic ritual performed during the gathering. For instance, in curing fever, the herbalist pulls stinging nettles—roots and all—out of the soil while calling the name of the sick person. He avoids a mistaken identity by also invoking the name of the patient's parents.

Another ancient belief holds that like cures like. For example, blood root (potentilla erecta) has blood-red colored rhizomes, and thus allegedly can heal blood diseases. Several yellow-colored blossoming plants were the accepted remedies against jaundice. Sassafras (saxifraga) was the prescription for bladder stones. Burstwort (herniaria glabra) was the prescription for hernias. Eye Bright (euphrasia) was the treatment for eye diseases.

Until the eighteenth century, there was no difference between herbalists and physicians; the herbalists were physicians. With the industrial revolution came the scientific revolution. Physicians and pharmacists learned to analyze the components of plants, to isolate them, and finally to reproduce them synthetically. Chemical preparations began their triumphal march, accompanied by the enthusiasm of entire generations, who hoped to get better and faster relief and healing. The ancient art of preparing remedies from plants was lost.

The pharmaceutical industry is big business; only the weapons industry is bigger. Pharmaceutical companies rely on their knowledge of the active ingredients of plants; they cannot patent the entire plant, only its active ingredients. Their interest is in isolating the active ingredients in these plants in order to reproduce them synthetically. Thus, they only need to explain to the doctors and patients that the synthetic preparations are better and less dangerous than the natural ones.

In the last few years, however, the pendulum has swung back. Gradually it has dawned on us that a healing herb is most effective in its entirety. The scientific revolution has removed life and soul from the cosmos. The fragrance and beauty of plants have as much effect on one's well-being as their essences and active agents.

How to Prepare Herbal Medicine

Nature has provided an herb for each disease. Herbs comfort body and soul. Because they contain their active ingredients in the exact combination that our bodies need to regain their health, herbs often offer better help than do their chemical components. If you want to prepare herbal medicines for minor ailments, you can do so. In case you want to collect and dry healing plants for yourself, you find some advice for the best timing on page 86.

A caveat: not all healing plants are harmless. Many have unknown and dangerous side effects. Confine yourself to simple recipes for small ailments, with which you cannot make any mistakes. Do not experiment! If you do not get better, see a physician. You can try the following recipes without any risks.

Herbs have different applications. The following are a few that laymen can prepare without difficulty.

Infusions and Strong Herbal Teas

Prepare as you would a regular tea:

- Pour one cup of boiling water over a rounded tablespoon of herbs. Steep.
- Blossoms usually only need a few minutes.
- Leaves and seeds should steep 20 to 30 minutes so that all the active ingredients are extracted.

Decoction

This is made from the hard parts of a healing plant, such as roots, bark, seeds, and stems:

- Put the plant parts in cold water.
- Bring to a boil.
- Simmer for at least 15 minutes on low heat so that the active ingredients are available.
- Especially hard pieces take even longer.

Hot Poultice

- Dip a clean linen bandage in a decoction or an infusion.
- Wring out until just moist.
- Place over the ailing body part.

Ointments

- Take 8 parts of petroleum jelly or other soft fat.
- Mix with 2 parts of herbs (for example, marigold flowers).
- Heat while mixing thoroughly.

Hot Compresses

- Make a soft, clean, cloth bag the same size as the body part you want to cover.
- Fill with herbs.
- Pour boiling water over it.
- Squeeze the compress in a clean towel to remove excess fluid.
- Use the compress as hot as you can endure it.
- This is good for nerve pain, and painful joints and muscles. It also gives rise to refreshing sleep when placed on the stomach.

Home Remedies from Herb Lore

Herbal remedies can be used for the following common ailments:

First-Degree Burns

- Make a compress out of comfrey, mustard, and yarrow. This gives relief.

Low Fever

- Chamomile and yarrow tea are fever reducers. The theory is that these teas sipped every 30 minutes can normalize a fever within twenty-four hours.

Low Blood Pressure

- Pour hot water over marigold blossoms, steep for one hour, then strain. Sweeten with a little honey. Its effects are refreshing!

Sore Throat

- Prepare a tea made of three tablespoons of dried sage and 1 pint of hot water. Steep for 15 minutes and sip half a cup four times a day. Gargle with it as often as you like.

Cough

- Sipping rosemary tea, hot foot baths, and the juice of a raw or cooked onion are decongestants.
- You can also break up coriander, mix it with honey, and swallow it.

Mosquito Bites

- Parsley rubbed on the skin repels mosquitoes.

Wasp and Bee Stings

- Crush the leaves of melissa (balm). Put it on the sting. This relieves the pain.

Nervousness

- A bath made from lavender blossoms relaxes without making one tired. Fill a small cloth bag with blossoms and hang it under your water faucet while you fill the bathtub.

Headache

- Open the window, lie down for a while, and drink hot peppermint tea sweetened with honey. Also helpful is a hot foot bath to which you add a tablespoon of mustard herb.

Toothache

- Put yarrow directly on the painful tooth. This relieves the pain.

Tummy Ache

- Since the beginning of time, fennel tea is a miracle remedy against gas and heartburn.

Table 10
Moon Rules for Health

Activity	*Moon*		*Quarter*	*Zodiac sign*
	Waxing	*Waning*		
Birth Control	according to the personal moon sign of the woman			
Collecting Herbs (blossoms and leaves)	X		1, 2	Scorpio
Collecting Herbs (stems and roots)		X	3, 4	Scorpio
Conceive a baby	according to the personal moon sign of the woman		son in a masculine sign, daughter in feminine sign	
Detoxification		X	3, 4	
Deworming		X	3, 4	
Diuretics		X	3, 4	
Filling Teeth		X	3, 4	Taurus, Leo, Scorpio, Aquarius

Activity	*Moon*		*Quarter*	*Zodiac sign*
Fruit and Juice days		X	3, 4	
Health Cure	X		1, 2	
Oral Surgery		X	3, 4	not with moon in Taurus
Pulling Teeth	X		1, 2	Gemini, Virgo, Pisces, Sagittarius
Quit Alcohol		X	3, 4	
Quit Smoking		X	3, 4	Gemini, Leo, Virgo
Remove Warts		X	3, 4	
Stimulants & Vitamin Boost	X		1, 2	
Surgery	not at full moon or new moon plus or minus two days		not when the moon is in a sign that rules the body part having the surgery	
Treatment for Drug Addiction		X	3, 4	Gemini, Leo, Virgo
Weaning	X		1, 2	
Weight Gain	X		1, 2	Cancer, Scorpio, Pisces
Weight Loss		X	3, 4	Aries, Leo, Sagittarius

The Moon and Beauty

Carmen Waldstein is a Munich cosmetician and naturopath. Surprisingly, many cards in her customer files included the client's natal chart. At the very least, the customer's moon sign at birth is in the column beside her birthday and telephone number. This is how Carmen knows exactly what her customers need.

Carmen readily explains the reason for this unusual practice. A customer can only enjoy her whole treatment when her unique characteristics are taken into account. Only then is the treatment successful.

Someone who knows about astrology can easily read unique characteristics from a horoscope. The sun sign and rising sign dominate an interpretation of the character of a person. However, Carmen explains, in a feminine subject such as beauty and cosmetics, the moon sign is often more important than the sun sign. An Aries moon woman needs completely different treatment than does a Libra moon woman. Carmen's lovely, humorous typing of moon women and beauty treatments are listed below. In case you don't recognize yourself in the following, who knows? Perhaps in your case the sun sign dominates.

Moon Women and Cosmetics

Moon in Aries

These are usually women who do not like to go in for a treatment. They never come for a pleasant session. They only come in an emergency when they have problems with their skin that they cannot quickly fix themselves. Of course, they do not come regularly. If a treatment is unavoidable, then they sit in the comfortable treatment chair as if it were hot coals. Quick! Quick! We have only a little time! No masque and, of course, no massage!

This is a waste of time. A quick treatment of the problem area is all they can endure, and then they are gone!

Moon in Taurus

Women with a moon in Taurus are absolute connoisseurs. Whenever they can afford it, they regularly come for treatment. This is a luxury that they delight in. They enjoy everything you do for them. Fragrant masques that work into the skin for a long time, extensive massages, new makeup; they are delighted when you offer them a cup of coffee.

Moon in Gemini

Cosmetics are fine, but they must come with conversation. For Gemini moon women, the beauty shop is a place for communication, where you can also talk about beauty. Of course, they also do not take any new kind of treatment without commenting on it. First they want to know exactly what is being done to them and why. When they finally leave the beauty shop, the feeling of having had a good chat is as important to them as having soft skin and new makeup.

Moon in Cancer

These are the real moon women. The moon is Cancer's ruling planet. Therefore, these women especially enjoy pampering their skin. The atmosphere of the beauty shop is equally important to them. Cancer moon women need to feel comfortable with their cosmeticians. These moon women often suffer from water retention; lymph massage would especially suit them.

Moon in Leo

These are customers who want coddling. Their cosmetician has to concentrate only on them. They pout when the phone rings to interrupt their treatment. Style and outer appearance are very important to them; they would never leave the shop after a treatment without perfect makeup. Because Leo women often show a masculine side, they are very sensitive when the tiniest wrinkle appears. They buy every new wrinkle cream, and do everything to perfect their appearance; they want to be ready to compete in the career world.

Moon in Virgo

Virgo moon customers are friendly but naturally suspicious. They have to know the details about each step. If the cosmetician suggests a treatment with ampoules to a Virgo moon woman, the professional will have to convince her of its benefits. Then the Virgo moon client will make sure that she gets a new ampoule and not the leavings of an old one. They are also extremely accurate. They complain about pimples and skin disorders that you really cannot see. After the skin treatment, the skin should be deeply clean. Makeup, however, is not necessary.

Moon in Libra

Before a Libra moon customer comes into the beauty shop, the cosmetician who treats her has to make her self beautiful. People who do not look their best have no chance with a Libra moon woman. For the Libra moon woman, a cultivated, elegant appearance is a must. This is of importance for themselves, but they also do not accept uncultivated or unattractive appearance in other people. Libra moon women belong to that category of customer who appreciates regular treatments. They come as often as they can afford it. They do not care about the details of the treatment, however. The main thing is that they look excellent afterward.

Moon in Scorpio

Scorpio moon women are concerned about ecology and nature. They prefer to bring their own home concoctions, creams, and masques—or those from the ecology shop—to the treatment. These usually are pleasantly fragrant because of the natural ingredients, and have good quality. (This is not surprising, because Scorpio moon women are usually reincarnations of wise women who prepared their herbal mixtures themselves.) They do not think that beauty is as important as a cultivated, outer appearance. If makeup, then please make it as natural as possible!

Moon in Sagittarius

These are women with high expectations. When they go for a beauty treatment, one should be able to tell the difference afterwards. They seldom step into a beauty shop in order to relax or feel comfortable. They want to see a result—meaning an immediate positive change. How this happens and what it costs is not their concern. They are happy if someone tells them after the treatment "Today you look especially good!"

Moon in Capricorn

These are the women with real skin problems. Skin is their subject (see page 104 "Which Sign of the Zodiac Rules Which Part of the Body"). Therefore, Capricorn women often work as cosmeticians or as dermatologists. Capricorn moon women are reliable, pleasant customers. They come for treatment regularly, and are grateful for help and understanding. However, they do not come for enjoyment—only for practical reasons. It has to be because of their skin problems!

Moon in Aquarius

At each treatment you must offer something new to Aquarius moon women. They love to experiment and would like to look completely different every time. They are usually well-informed in the field of cosmetics, have read something about a new masque, or a new treatment method, in a women's magazine, and now they would like to try it. Fortunately, Aquarius moon women do not sulk if the treatment they requested does not make them more beautiful.

Moon in Pisces

Pisces moon women tend, like Capricorn women, to have skin problems. However, in contrast to the latter, they like the treatment in a beauty shop. If they get used to one beauty shop and cosmetician, they are courteous, devoted, and loyal. They become regular customers, not only because of their sensitive skin.

Did you know?

Chamomile Tea for Skin Impurities

Chamomile tea is a nearly universal beauty treatment.

- Pour boiling water over dried chamomile.
- Use one pint of hot water for one ounce of chamomile.
- Steep for three to four hours.
- Strain and use as a facial lotion.
- It remains fresh in the refrigerator for approximately one week.
- Chamomile tea as a rinse for blond hair gives it shine.

Did you know?

Strawberries for Beauty

Strawberries have cosmetic value.

- Strawberry juice can augment the healing of different skin diseases such as eczema and itching.
- Cigarette stains on teeth can be bleached with strawberry juice.

Beauty Treatments According to the Moon

The moon determines the method of a beauty treatment. Not all lunar phases are suitable for all kinds of beauty treatments. Of course, no beauty shop can afford to work only at particular lunar phases, but luckily, this is not necessary. Certain routine treatments, such as cleansing, purifying, facial masques, massage, and makeup, are good for skin (and for soul) in each lunar position. For other treatments, Carmen Waldstein schedules appointments for the right time without long explanations. She picks a date when the treatment might have the greatest success.

The waxing moon is a good time for exfoliation, deep cleansing, and for removing blackheads, whiteheads, pimples, and skin impurities. During a waxing moon, the skin is moist, plump, and with good circulation—particularly at full moon. At this time, the skin is especially open and receptive. Naturally, the impurities come to the surface from the inside. It is easy to remove them, and afterwards the lesion is nearly invisible.

During a waning moon, the skin is much drier. When you remove skin problems, you have to take into account that, in spite of good care, the lesion can become inflamed and can even scar. The most difficult time is at the new moon. According to Carmen, no pimple or blackhead wants to come out! The new moon and the entire waning phase is a good time to detoxify the skin and to do treatments that could be painful—facelifts, permanent makeup, and removal of skin problems. At this time, there is less circulation in the skin and it is less sensitive to pain.

Manicures According to the Moon

According to magical tradition, the moon governs the fingernails. Trim them during a waning moon so that they do not grow back as quickly. The ideal time for this is while the moon is in Sagittarius, Taurus, Cancer, or Leo.

The best time to remove calluses is while the moon is in the third or fourth quarter.

Did you know?

Dill Liquid Strengthens the Fingernails

The mineral salts and high acid level in dill make it an excellent treatment for strengthening fingernails.

- Take two teaspoons of crushed dill seed and two teaspoons of chopped horsetail.
- Add one cup of water.
- Simmer until half of the liquid has boiled away.
- Cool to body temperature.
- Soak fingernails in it for about a quarter of an hour, preferably during a waxing moon.
- Repeat until the nails have become visibly stronger.
- The liquid keeps fresh in the refrigerator for about one week.

Cosmetic Surgery

The best time to have cosmetic surgery is during a waning moon, preferably when it does not square or oppose Mars. Of course, the moon should not be in a sign which rules the body part that is having the surgery. For example, do not have rhinoplasty while the moon is in Scorpio; do not have ears pinned back while the moon is in Taurus.

Did you know?

Skin—The Mirror of the Soul

When people are sensitive to the moon, you can even see the moon phases in their skin. An unusually blatant example is the tragic story told in Llewellyn's Moon Sign Book. A woman was radiantly beautiful as long as the moon was waxing. As soon as the full moon passed, she shriveled up and became wrinkled and ugly. For two weeks out of every month, she could not show herself! Cancer women are especially sensitive to the changes of the moon because the moon is the ruling planet over their sun sign. At new moon, their skin is ashy with poor circulation. During a waxing moon, their skin becomes rosy, clear, and vital.

Hair Depilatories

With hot wax or an electric depilatory, (such as Epilady™) the easiest and least painful hair removal is during a waxing moon. The best time is the full moon, when the hair follicles are full and stimulated. However, someone very sensitive to pain would be better off using depilatories during a waning moon, when the hair grows back more slowly and the effects last longer.

Did you know?

Ideal Dates for Beauty Masques

If you want to give yourself a treat, do a masque on Taurus and Libra moon days. Then the effects are more noticeable and longer lasting.

The Moon and Hair

Hair problems are not just a modern concern. Moon Rules for hair have been passed down to us through the centuries; some are thousands of years old. These rules state the ideal dates for washing, cutting, and dying hair. For example, the Roman emperor Tiberius (32 B.C. to A.D. 37) ordered his barber to come only during a waxing moon. He hoped that his hair would grow stronger and faster. Since those days, countless similar stories have been told about the laws of lunar sympathy. These concur that everything grows better during a waxing moon than during a waning moon.

The Moon and Hair Care

- Dark hair cut at the full moon becomes lighter.
- Haircuts in Taurus become shaggy.
- Never cut hair while the moon is in Capricorn; it turns gray prematurely.
- If the hairstyle needs to last longer, then cut it during a waning moon; it will grow out more slowly.
- When hair should grow faster, cut it in the moon signs of Gemini, Aquarius, and Libra.
- For a permanently curly crowning glory, cut the hair while the moon is in Aries (preferably waxing). For a man, the recommended moon sign is Leo.
- Wash hair in the favorable water signs of Cancer and Scorpio.
- Haircuts are best while the moon is in a mutable sign (Gemini, Virgo, Sagittarius, Pisces) or in an earth sign (Taurus, Capricorn)
- For faster hair growth, a water sign is ideal for cutting.
- For thicker hair, cut it while the moon is in opposition to the sun or at the full moon.
- If hair needs to grow slowly, cut it preferably in Gemini or Leo during a waning moon, preferably while Saturn is squared or in opposition to the moon.

- Permanents, hair relaxants, or dyes are best in Aquarius.

The American astrologer Linda Goodman makes a suggestion in her book *Starsigns:*

> *No matter whether you are a woman or a man, if you want to have your hair short and do not want to go too often to the beautician because it is too expensive or time consuming, then have it cut regularly on a full moon day. It will grow much slower. Capricorns, Taureans, Virgoans, this saves you a lot of money! If, however, you have cut off your hair and you regret it and cannot wait until it grows out again, trim it at each new moon just a tad. If you do not trust your beautician, you can do it yourself. It is only important to cut your hair regularly at the new moon. Then you will realize that your hair is growing much faster.*

Haircutting According to the Moon—the Latest

To bring some light to this confusing pile of rules, Munich hairstylist Georg Hirschbolz made some interesting observations. For fifteen years, he worked according to the moon phases. He is fifty years old, and has a real lion's mane.

Fifteen years ago, Georg Hirschbolz became interested in the Moon Rules. His interest began when a young customer came into his shop to have her ends trimmed. She complained bitterly about her hair. It was too fine and did not want to grow. The long hairstyle that she had dreamed of for a long time would probably remain an eternal dream. Hirschbolz only could agree. He had to admit that he did not know any miracle cure for this problem.

Then, the customer in the neighboring chair joined the conversation. She suggested, "Why don't you get a haircut during a waxing moon, preferably the third day after the new moon or the third day before the full moon? Then hair grows faster and thicker. My mother used to do this when we were children. In those days, we also had very thin hair." The maestro inspected this woman's strong hair and decided to give it a try. He had nothing to lose. Also, unlike most of his colleagues, he liked long hair.

So Georg bought a simple moon calendar. He marked these two days in his appointment book: the third day after the new moon and the third day before the full moon. He began to schedule customers who wanted long hair for these days. Of course, among these was the young girl with the thin hair. The first obvious successes came faster than expected, and especially with children. During the following months, short, thin hair grew to midlength with much stronger hair shafts. However, Georg admits that "fast" is a relative term. It takes about a year to grow any customer's short hair to shoulder length.

On the average, hair grows a little less than half an inch a month. The moon cannot significantly change the rate of growth. However, trimming the artfully grown inches of hair does not sacrifice the length. Hirschbolz's hair salon technique does not square off the ends; they only get a slight trim. Thus, damaged and limp ends are snipped without changing the length of the hair. Healthy, strong hair grows back.

Inspired by this visible success and the growing number of customers who wanted to keep or grow long hair (and no longer had to fear losing a millimeter at each visit to the stylist), Georg studied all the available literature on the moon and hair. He began to test what he read in his business to see if it was valid. Today, fifteen years later, these are his experiences.

Hair is an energy carrier. It shows whether its owner is in good or bad physical or psychological health. If the person feels well, his hair has shine, body, and is manageable. A person who does not feel well has tired, lifeless hair. The best haircut cannot change this. Hair is as sensitive as its owner and needs a certain vibration in order to feel well. The best day for cutting is the third day after the new moon and the third day before the full moon. On these days, the hair does not lose any energy. This does not mean that all customers have to stand in line for these two days in the month. People with healthy, thick hair do not have to follow this schedule. Healthy hair can easily take minor energy loss during trimming.

According to Hirschbolz, it is important that women who desire long hair be aware of vibrations. His role model is American physician and hair specialist Dr. George Michael (internationally known as the Long Hair Pope). He devoted himself to women with long hair and formulated the theory that hair grows along so-called positive and negative lines. The line from the crown of the head to the first vertebra is positive. The line from the first vertebra to the end of the nape is negative. The line from the shoulder line to between the shoulder blades is positive.

In the positive lines, a good haircut falls beautifully. Just shake your head, and the style falls back into place. It becomes critical, however, when hair grows out of the positive into the negative line. If hair rests on the shoulders, it cannot move freely in its vibrational field because something is always in its way (e.g., the collar or the shoulders). Then problems start; the hair becomes sick and the ends split. However, once the length is past the shoulders, the hair problems are over. The vibration is all right! Customers whose hair has not yet reached this dream length can overcome this awkward stage quickly. They can regularly trim the ends on the two best moon days.

It does not matter whether people with short, normal hair, which grows within the positive lines, have their hair styled during the waxing or waning moon, although Moon Rules suggest otherwise. Georg says, "This might have played a role in the olden days, when hair was cut according to the French method. People who want to save money these days do not usually come during a waning moon; they hope that the hair might grow more slowly (although it does grow a little). Customers who are short on cash just come less frequently to get their hair cut. This is all right, because now most good hairstylists know the English precision cut. A perfect haircut will fall into place, even after a few months, as long as it grows in the positive zone. However, if this line is grown over, only another precision cut can help." The expert is sure about this point. Fifteen years of experience speak for themselves. But he is still experimenting. He has a theory that he finds very interesting. When men get haircuts regularly in the sign of

Leo, their hair improves and becomes stronger. "For ten years, whenever the moon was in Leo, a customer came in regularly of his own volition. I remember that in the beginning he had fine, straight hair. Since then, he has grown a real lion's mane. Even the structure of this hair changed. Today it has a slight wave." Hirschbolz is fascinated, but does not yet dare generalize these observations.

Did you know?

Rosemary Enlivens the Hair

- Prepare a liquid from rosemary leaves and boiling water.
- Steep for about one hour.
- Strain it and use it as a hair rinse.
- Preferably do this during a waxing moon, when the scalp is more porous.
- Rosemary stimulates the scalp (also the facial skin) and strengthens limp hair.

Permanents

Georg still is experimenting with permanents according to the moon phases. He can already testify that perms given during a Virgo moon stay especially well in long hair and have great bounce. Conversely, slipups happen more often on Leo moon days than during other moon signs. For example, a customer might have a failed perm that is too frizzy.

Hair Color

Customers who color their hair with plant dyes have good results during a waxing moon. At that time, the hair is especially absorbent.

Did you know?

Stinging Nettles for Gray Hair

Rinse the hair with stinging nettle liquid. This makes gray hair darker naturally. Use one handful of nettles to a quart of boiling water.

Shampoo and Grooming

The old rule used to be, do not wash hair too often, it will get too greasy. This is no longer valid today. The scalp has to be clean and free from pollution and toxins. The biological balance must be correct for hair to feel good. If hairs feel uncomfortable for a long time, they die because they do not want to stick around. They fall out in handfuls. Thus, you should shampoo frequently but correctly. A mild shampoo is important. Do not just slap it onto the top of your head in the shower. Massage the shampoo gently and thoroughly into the scalp. Let it soak, then rinse completely.

Table 11
Moon Rules for Beauty

Activity	*Moon*		*Quarter*	*Zodiac sign*
	Waxing	*Waning*		
Bio face lift, Permanent makeup, minor surgery		X	3, 4	
Hair cut, long hair, thin hair	X	three days after the new moon or three days before full moon	1, 2	
Hair cut, spars hair				Leo
Hair dying	X		1, 2	
Manicure		X	3, 4	Cancer, Leo, Taurus, Sagittarius
Masques	X		1, 2	Libra
Permanents	X		1, 2	Virgo
Removing pimples, blackheads & whiteheads	X		1, 2	

Part III

Your Personal Moon—
Moon Rules for Family,
Career and Everyday Life

Moon and Character

Experience has shown that the closest celestial bodies have a definite influence on the weather, vegetation, etc. One can only ascend step by step and cannot say when this effect seizes... . I won't even call this and similar illusions superstition. It is quite close to our human nature and is the same as any belief.

J.W. von Goethe to F. Schiller in 1798

Even those who do not want to have anything to do with astrology, and who consider the Moon Rules to be fairy tales, know which sign of the zodiac to read when they check their daily horoscope in the newspaper which—of course—they are only doing for the fun of it.

In newspapers, you always find your sun sign, not because it says the most, but because it is the easiest to find out. The slow-moving sun stays for approximately one month in each zodiac sign. Newspapers usually list in parentheses when each sign begins and ends, so that anyone who knows his birthday can see at a glance where the sun was at the time of his birth. Obviously, this is how most people do it. Even though everyone ridicules the horoscope, newspapers realize they cannot afford to omit such a column. Recent polls found that 65 percent of adult Germans regularly read their horoscopes—a rating that most other sections only dream of.

Table 12
How to Find Your Sun Sign

Sign	*Symbol*	*Date*
Aries	♈	21 March to 20 April
Taurus	♉	21 April to 21 May
Gemini	♊	22 May to 21 June
Cancer	♋	22 June to 22 July
Leo	♌	23 July to 23 August
Virgo	♍	24 August to 23 September
Libra	♎	24 September to 23 October
Scorpio	♏	24 October to 22 November
Sagittarius	♐	23 November to 21 December
Capricorn	♑	22 December to 20 January
Aquarius	♒	21 January to 18 February
Pisces	♓	19 February to 20 March

Sometimes the date in which the sun enters or leaves a sign shifts about one day. The reason is the same as for the leap year. Each day is one minute longer than twenty-four hours. If you are born on the first or last day of your sign, it is safer to find your sun sign through a natal chart.

Did you know?

The Invention of the Newspaper Horoscope

The brief horoscope based on sun signs is not very old. British astrologer R.N. Naylor invented this popular horoscope shortly before the second World War. After he became famous by predicting the accident of airship R-101 in 1930, the London *Sunday Express* asked him to write a regular feature about astrology. Naylor had the idea to divide the readers into twelve groups according to their sun signs and write a prediction for each group. Such a simplification would have made any classical astrologers' hair stand on end. Indeed, astrology is anything but simple.

How Astrology Works

Astrology tries to make an orderly pattern out of the seemingly accidental occurrences of everyday life. In order to do this, it reduces the multitude of events into twelve archetypal principles. Their symbols are the twelve signs of the zodiac. Not only the zodiac signs but also the houses (areas of living) are important in a person's chart. The planets (the dynamic part of the zodiac) and the aspects (relationships between the planets) also play a major role.

Anyone who knows something about astrology knows that sun signs are only the tip of the astrological iceberg. In the natal chart, the three primary astrological influences are the sun (personality), rising sign (life purpose), and the moon (emotions). The characteristics of the moon sign are the basic qualities of the personality that directly influence instinctive behavior. The moon shows how we react emotionally, from the gut. Feeling, instinct, motherliness—men and women depend on these vibrations from time to time. A person's moon indicates the vibrational level.

The rising sign (ascendant) and moon sign are not as easy to find as the sun sign. This is because the moon enters a new sign every two to three days, and the ascendant changes signs every two hours. It is no wonder that the sun sign has become so popular for those who want to know something about themselves without too much effort.

By the way, this approach is not as meaningless as most serious astrologers might think at first. Of course, it is absurd to predict on the basis of their sun sign that one twelfth of the population will find Thursday to be short on domestic bliss, or that next Tuesday will be a good day to ask for a pay raise. Sun sign astrology has something to say about a person's character, but it only takes into account one aspect. You may not identify with the description of your sun sign personality for a number of different reasons:

- You have put too much faith in those newspaper horoscopes, which are generalized nonsense. Do not confuse them with true astrology.
- The description is accurate, but you are not willing to admit that certain traits fit your personality. This happens more often that one likes to admit.
- Your moon sign has an effect on your sun sign. This happens often, especially when emotions play a role. The moon sign is more expressive than the sun sign, especially for so-called lunar types. Based on its position in the natal chart, the moon influences these people very intensely. Cancers and those born during a full moon or a new moon are especially influenced by the moon.

Did you know?

The United States is a Cancerean Country

This country celebrates its birthday on 4 July, meaning that its sun sign is Cancer. Cancer's ruling planet is the moon. The areas of emotion, family, children, home, and security are especially important to Americans. Americans get ribbed for these qualities, but they cannot help it; they have learned them from the cradle.

What Type of Moon Person Are You?

The moon determines your instinctive reactions to certain situations. A person has a "moon reaction" before he thinks. Your moon sign shows how spontaneous you are and reveals your capacity for empathy and respect for other's emotions. The moon sign defines early childhood, relationship to the mother, natural trust, and relationships with women. You can read about the main characteristics of the twelve moon types according to the signs of the zodiac in the following table. You can also check whether or not these descriptions fit you and the people you know. If you do not know your moon sign, you can calculate it according to Table 8 on page 112. The exact sign may differ from the one you find in this table by about one sign. If you want to be accurate, you will have to cast your natal horoscope.

The Moon in the Signs of the Zodiac

Moon in Aries
Ruling planet—Mars; cardinal fire sign.

In a few words: dynamic, active, ready and capable of carrying things through, ambitious, independent, alert, enthusiastic, in-

spiring; also impatient, undisciplined, thick-headed, intolerant, fickle.

People with an Aries moon think that they are wonderful. Full of enthusiasm, they jump on anything new and feel convinced no one else is as qualified for the endeavor as they are. It does not matter whether it is in sports, career, war, or love. Aries moon people put all their eggs in one basket. Sometimes they put their heads through a wall. Unfortunately, they are involved in so many engagements that patience and perseverance are not their strong points, and discipline is out of the question. When Aries moon people blow their wad of enthusiasm, they lose interest and drop whatever they are doing. They hate routine, and cultivated laziness is a nightmare to them—also aging, because there is nothing they can do about it!

Moon in Taurus

Ruling planet—Venus; fixed earth sign

In a few words: consistent, down-to-earth, close to nature, practical, stubborn, thoroughly considers things of interest and then sticks to his opinion, family-oriented, sensuous, often musical, creative, materialistic.

The impulsive and changeable moon is most harmonious in the quiet sign of Taurus. Taurus moon people have sunny dispositions. They are always concerned with their own well-being and that of their loved ones. Money does not play a big role for most of them. They work with their money very skillfully so that they always have enough. If it happens that they do not succeed, they initially feel completely confused and deeply depressed; then they manage to come up with enough money for an elegant meal. Taurus moon people love to be mothered. In turn, they are very caring and loving family people. Weaknesses? Well! They are a little stubborn, a little pig-headed and phlegmatic, and if you provoke them, they really see red. God bless their opponents, because Taurus moon people take a long time to calm down. Nobody's perfect!

Moon in Gemini

Ruling planet—Mercury, mutable air sign

In a few words: smart, curious, alert, talkative, quick-witted, intellectual: also always restless, jumpy, nervous, mercurial, easily bored.

Gemini moon people often are more intensely Gemini than people with the sun in Gemini. This may be because the moon stimulates them to intuitive, spontaneous reactions. They do have brains, but they take these for granted. Gemini moon people are brilliant salesmen, travel agents, teachers, and journalists. For them, communication is vital. Language is their life's elixir. They formulate with enthusiasm. They are witty, amusing, and the life of the party. If you do not find them at a party, you may find them on the telephone. They have to stay in contact—with whom it doesn't matter. Change is necessary in all things; otherwise they become bored easily. They are tolerant, uncomplicated, and jolly. Only stupidity gets on their nerves.

Moon in Cancer

Ruling planet—Moon; cardinal water sign

In a few words: caring, warmhearted, imaginative, sensible, emotional, homey: also hypersensitive, moody, easily hurt.

Cancer is a sign ruled by the moon. Moon in Cancer emphasizes the qualities of the moon—often more than in sun in Cancer. Moon Cancers are more sensible and more sensitive, but also moodier than sun Cancers. Home and family are an absolute must. For family members, this has advantages, because the warm, cuddly and secure atmosphere is very nourishing. There are also disadvantages. Cancer moon people tend to cling, but woe if they feel misunderstood! Traumatic events within the family weigh on them more than on other moon signs. Sometimes it takes years for them to cope with a tragedy such as divorce or death. Cancer moon people love to travel. They love new and different things, but they highly appreciate returning to their own four walls after the trip.

Moon in Leo
Ruling Planet—Sun; fixed fire sign

In a few words: youthful, playful, loves children, sunny, charming, generous, loyal to their friends, dignified, hard-working especially in the creative field: also slightly pompous, melodramatic, domineering and dogmatic.

Leo's ruling planet is the sun. Thus, compared with other signs, this sign subdues the moon's qualities. Leo moon people have strong feelings for others as well as for themselves. They need to hear from time to time that they are the greatest. If nobody tells them this, they may tell it to themselves and believe it. What would a Leo be without his pathos? However, it is easy to forgive him. His warm, sunny attitude does not let anyone get too angry with him. One can also forgive his sometimes exaggerated love of luxury. However, he has a tendency to think that he knows everything better than others. He has a degree of self-satisfaction and God-given egotism with which he always pushes himself into the foreground. He also tends to demand more understanding from his fellows than he would ever be able to muster himself.

Moon in Virgo
Ruling Planet—Mercury; mutable earth sign

In a few words: shy, introverted, perfectionist, hard-working, matter-of-fact, businesslike, outwardly cool, inwardly very often nervous and too anxious, strong but controlled feelings.

Virgo moon people nearly burst from longing to be used. They rarely complain and are extremely painstaking. In their brief periods of free time, they repair their friend's car, fix their neighbor's broken zipper, mow the lawn without being asked, and spring clean—as long as they may complain afterwards that they are over burdened. However, they never ask of anyone more than they themselves are ready to give. Their industriousness is legendary. Nothing makes them happier than being reassured that they are absolutely irreplaceable. The feeling of being needed is the only feeling to which they will admit. This is because they are not so good at tenderness or serenity. From childhood on, they strive to get affection through the qualities of reason and achievement. They were adults almost before they were born.

Moon in Libra
Ruling Planet—Venus; cardinal air sign

In a few words: harmonious, peaceful, charming, diplomatic, balanced, loving, romantic, aesthetics are important, must be surrounded by beauty, brilliant theorist but has difficulty putting good ideas into practice: also ambitious, willful, indecisive, wavering, moody.

People with a Libra moon are born diplomats. Style, taste, charm, and courtesy have been theirs from birth. If they display these qualities, they put their best feet forward; it is a delight to be with them as long as their surroundings can keep the appearance of an ideal world of harmony and joy. If this does not work out, then Libra moon people disappear. They have very limited tolerance for discordance; if things get worse than their tolerance threshold (which is pretty low), they cannot stand it. They need partners who compliment them for their psychological balance—the other side of the scales, as it were. They need harmony. If a partner cannot give this to them, then too bad! They immediately have to look for someone else who knows how to appreciate their ideal of harmony.

Moon in Scorpio
Ruling Planet—Pluto; fixed water sign

In a few words: reliable, industrious, determined, independent, strong, intense, passionate, very loving to close people: also reserved, easily irritated, revengeful.

People with a Scorpio moon do not make things easy on themselves nor on their environment. In the positive as well as the negative sense, they are intense, passionate, and do not rest until they have penetrated the deepest, most hidden emotions. They simply accept that they may create suffering with their passion. When hurt, they are extremely vengeful—far beyond every reasonable measure and even if it is self-destructive. Most of them, however, also have the ability to heal. With their innate intensity, they are not afraid to violate taboos.

Moon in Sagittarius
Ruling Planet—Jupiter; mutable fire sign

In a few words: optimistic, open-minded, enthusiastic, eloquent, freedom-loving, independent, active, philosophical, intuitive, talented, lively: also impatient, restless, careless to the point of thoughtlessness, pleasure seeking, exhibitionist.

People with a Sagittarius moon are enthusiastic about everything: culture, travel, philosophy, sports, politics, and all great ideas. They love a challenge. Because of their quick analytical minds, they are able to lead others. However, they always need someone to take care of the troublesome details. Education is basic for them. They have little patience for people who are slower than they but who nevertheless question their lofty thoughts. Their problem is their restlessness, which makes them jump from one project to the next. Everything that threatens mobility frightens them. This includes whatever ties them to the house, such as family, children, and property. However, they soon find the ideal solution to this problem: a motor home, baby-sitter, travel crib, or buggy so that they can carry the little ones wherever they go. Thus, they bring change and stimulation into family life from the start. Children with Sagittarius moon parents grow up in museums, art expositions, lecture halls, on trips, and on the tennis court.

Moon in Capricorn
Ruling Planet—Saturn; cardinal earth sign

In a few words: serious, disciplined, ambitious, industrious, orderly, thorough, spartan, distant, clever in business.

People with a Capricorn moon are proud of their clear, practical common sense. In connection with their other qualities, such as ambition and discipline, this makes them very successful. Being too matter-of-fact and overly cautious can lead them to be short on the joy of living. In the social area, they tend to be insecure and reserved. They have very sensitive feelings. Because they cannot rationalize their feelings, they may find them frightening. Their severity, self-discipline, and austere way of life (so that later they will be better off) can make living with a Capricorn moon person difficult.

Moon in Aquarius
Ruling Planet—Uranus; fixed air sign

In a few words: exceptional, rebellious, unconventional, philanthropic, engaging, original, creative, unsettled, unpredictable, distant.

People born under this moon sign have charisma and contagious enthusiasm. Wherever there is a need for courage to go in a new direction, they are first in line. *Avant garde* fashion, revolutionary ideas, modern art, sexual revolution, but also drugs and radicalism are excellent ways for them to shock the middle class. They not only want to shock, but also wish to change society for the better. This means freedom, equality, and brotherhood for everyone! Strong emotions frighten them. Personally, they feel much more comfortable if they can keep a certain distance. In relationships, they always feel the need to preserve their freedom and cannot stand clinging.

Moon in Pisces
Ruling Planet—Neptune; mutable water sign

In a few words: gentle, compassionate, soft-hearted, mystic, hermit, loving, tend to sacrifice for others, sensitive, vulnerable, clairvoyant, strongly intuitive, imaginative: also lazy, gullible, impractical, malleable, indecisive.

People born in a Pisces moon are very emotional. They go entirely with their feelings, whether for good or ill. They always take on the underdog or seemingly hopeless case. To protect themselves from feeling hurt, they tend to develop addictions. Alcohol, drugs, and excessive eating may be temporary escapes from the daunting problems of life. On the other hand, spiritualism is a solution for many. Because they are often talented psychics, they succeed in finding acknowledgment, warmth, and security in the esoteric arena. The Pisces moon person cannot exist without these validations.

Did you know?

Children from One Mother Often Share the Same Moon Sign

Because the moon relates to the symbol of the mother, children of the same mother often have the same moon sign. At the very least, they usually have a moon sign from the same element (fire, air, water, earth).

The Moon Phase at Birth

Many astrologers are of the opinion that not only the moon sign but also the moon phase at the time of birth is very important to a person's personality. People who were born at the full moon are completely different from those who were born at the new moon or during a lunar eclipse. Of course, whether the moon was waning or waxing also plays a role. In the following section, you can read the characteristics of people born in the major moon phases. See if you can find yourself in the descriptions that follow.

How to Find Your Moon Phase

If you know your sun and your moon sign, you can use the following table (Table 13) to determine at a glance what the moon phase was when you were born. To do so, you need to know your moon sign and your sun sign.
If you do not know your moon sign, you can calculate it using Table 8 on page 112, Table 12 helps you find your sun sign.

Does the characteristics of the phase you find fit you?

Table 13

How to Find Your Moon Phase

Read the moon sign horizontally; the sun sign vertically. You will find the moon phase of your birth at the crossing point. Example: Cancer sun and Scorpio moon means that your birthday was in the second quarter.

Sun sign	First half: Waxing moon — Moon sign		Second half: Waning moon — Moon sign	
	1st quarter (new moon—waxing half moon)	2nd quarter (waxing half moon—full moon	3rd quarter (full moon—waning half moon)	4th quarter (waning half moon—new moon)
Aries	Aries, Taurus, Gemini	Cancer, Leo, Virgo, Libra	Scorpio, Sagittarius	Capricorn, Aries, Aquarius, Pisces
Taurus	Taurus, Gemini, Cancer	Leo, Virgo, Libra, Scorpio	Sagittarius, Capricorn	Aquarius, Pisces, Aries, Taurus
Gemini	Gemini, Cancer, Leo	Virgo, Libra, Scorpio, Sagittarius	Capricorn, Aquarius	Pisces, Aries, Taurus, Gemini
Cancer	Cancer, Leo, Virgo	Libra, Scorpio, Sagittarius, Capricorn	Aquarius, Pisces	Aries, Taurus, Gemini, Cancer
Leo	Leo, Virgo, Libra	Scorpio, Sagittarius, Capricorn, Aquarius	Pisces, Aries	Taurus, Gemini, Cancer, Leo
Virgo	Virgo, Libra, Scorpio	Sagittarius, Capricorn, Aquarius, Pisces	Aries, Taurus	Gemini, Cancer, Leo, Virgo

Sun sign	First half: Waxing moon		Second half: Waning moon	
	Moon sign		Moon sign	
	1st quarter (new moon—waxing half moon)	2nd quarter (waxing half moon—full moon	3rd quarter (full moon—waning half moon)	4th quarter (waning half moon—new moon)
Libra	Libra, Scorpio, Sagittarius	Capricorn, Aquarius, Pisces, Aries	Taurus, Gemini,	Cancer, Leo, Virgo, Libra
Scorpio	Scorpio, Sagittarius, Capricorn	Aquarius, Pisces, Aries, Taurus	Gemini, Cancer	Leo, Virgo, Libra, Scorpio
Sagittarius	Sagittarius, Capricorn, Aquarius	Pisces, Aries, Taurus, Gemini	Cancer, Leo	Virgo, Libra, Scorpio, Sagittarius
Capricorn	Capricorn, Aquarius, Pisces	Aries, Taurus, Gemini, Cancer	Leo, Virgo	Libra, Scorpio, Sagittarius, Capricorn
Aquarius	Aquarius, Pisces, Aries	Taurus, Gemini, Cancer, Leo	Virgo, Libra	Scorpio, Sagittarius, Capricorn, Aquarius
Pisces	Pisces, Aries, Taurus	Gemini, Cancer, Leo, Virgo	Libra, Scorpio	Sagittarius, Capricorn, Aquarius, Pisces

If You Were Born During the First Quarter

(New Moon to Waxing Half Moon)

No matter what your sun sign, you have something of an Aries in you: enthusiastic, stormy, and always searching for what is new. Your lifestyle expresses the fresh, young energy of the new moon. New beginnings are easy for you. You cannot help but set out with vitality and enthusiasm, bypassing those who were born with less energy. You also tend not to finish what you have started. When you begin to feel bored, you leave other people hanging. Let them finish the project! You are long gone to new ground, where the grass is much greener to your eyes.

If You Were Born During the Second Quarter

(Waxing Half Moon to Full Moon)

You are ambitious, focused, and feel the need to create something permanent. You are an achiever, and it is important that your achievements be acknowledged and appreciated. Even during your youth, you have good prospects for becoming successful. However, your ability to remain at the top depends on other factors in your horoscope. Because of your infectious personality, you will always find people around you to support your efforts to succeed. Although you do tend to reciprocate, your friends need to be aware that over the long run they will only get back some of what they put in. You are loving, kind, and charismatic, but also definitely an opportunist. The Leo in you cannot be overlooked.

If You Were Born During the Third Quarter

(Full Moon to Waning Half Moon)

You need a lot of personal contact. Friendship, family and colleagues play an important role in your life. The warmth that these relationships give you makes you strong. You can achieve a lot on your own, but without the support of friendship and the encouragement of others, you have only half your vitality. You enjoy not only your own success, but also supporting people you admire and helping them realize their goals. People who are more active, purposeful, and more energetic than you have your unlimited admiration. Besides, sex may play a very important role in your life. In this moon phase, Scorpio is evident. By the way, you can look forward to the second half of your life. The most successful time begins when you have passed the midpoint of your life.

If You Were Born During the Fourth Quarter (Waning Half Moon to New Moon)

Because you finish things that others have begun and solve problems that others have caused, you do not have time to start anything on your own. You pick the chestnuts out of the fire for everyone else. You do this very well because of your instinctively correct behavior. You would be very satisfied if you could just watch the world's activity without having to be too involved. You do not need much. Material things are not important. You obediently fulfill the duties that life has given you, but do not despair: late in life, at an age when most people have retired, you will experience a metamorphosis and will find success and acknowledgment in a completely new field.

The full moon and the new moon have a particularly intense effect on your destiny if you were born exactly at that moment. With respect to birth situations and life tasks, it appears that people who were born at the new moon are better off.

If You Were Born at the New Moon

You benefit from the extreme intensity of this lunar position. You are dynamic and efficient, but at the same time you radiate a certain naiveté everything is so new! You react with unusual emotion and impulsiveness. Again and again, this leads to problems. Your mother probably had an especially powerful influence in your life. Because at new moon the moon, which symbolizes the mother, is directly over the sun, which represents self-esteem, people born at the new moon may be overshadowed by a strong mother figure. The moon and the sun are conjunct at new moon (meaning, positioned in the same sign); thus, the new moon often represents the specific qualities of this sign. For example, if you are born at the new moon in the sign of Taurus, the qualities of Taurus are probably strongly emphasized in you.

If You Were Born at the Full Moon

Life is not always easy for people born under the full moon. Astrologers have observed two obvious types of personalities among those born at full moon: those who are close to enlightenment, and those who seem far from it (who are, at the very least, emotionally disturbed). This lunar position awakens opposite forces within such a person, who is torn between them. Which side will ultimately be victorious is unpredictable. People who succeed in integrating these rivaling needs have an unusual capacity to think clearly, and usually have no special problems in life. Quite the contrary! Whoever can handle this difficult birth situation can also succeed in everything else. People who are not able to do so, feel torn their whole lives and often suffer negative feelings that express themselves with special intensity and drama at the full moon. People born at the full moon have a special destiny. Their birth situation creates a precarious balance throughout their lives. They have a great sense of humor and the ability to laugh about conflicts—and also about themselves.

Did you know?

More Sons are Born at Full Moon

An American scientist recently found out that more males are born at the full moon, and more females at the new moon. If this is true, then the moon or the moon goddess must have something in mind...

What Gypsies Know About Moon Phases

Gypsies know a little bit more about many things than other people do. This includes the meaning of the lunar position at a person's birth. The following are a few ancient pearls of wisdom from the gypsies:

People Born in the First Quarter

General prognosis—they have a long life.

- First Day: very lucky.
- Second day: extremely lucky.
- Third day: influential friends.
- Fourth day: their luck fluctuates dramatically.
- Fifth and sixth day: their pride might lead to problems.
- Seventh day: they need to keep their wishes to themselves if they want them to come true.

People Born in the Second Quarter

General prognosis—they have better lives than their parents.

- First day: prosperity.
- Second day: easy life.
- Third day: a lot of money through traveling.
- Fourth and fifth day: charming.
- Sixth day: success drops into their laps.
- Seventh day: lots of friends.

People Born in the Third Quarter

General prognosis—they have problems, but can solve them through perseverance.

- First day: luck and success on another continent.
- Second day: success in business.
- Third day: success through intuition.

- Fourth day: courage.
- Fifth day: caution with money.
- Sixth and seventh day: great strength.

People Born in the Fourth Quarter

General prognosis—kind and honest.

- First day and second day: they love their home.
- Third day: reliability.
- Fourth day: overly sensitive.
- Fifth day: ideal parents.
- Sixth day and seventh day: loyalty brings them wealth.

The question is, what can you do with this knowledge? If you want to find out whether this ancient gypsy wisdom makes sense, you must try to figure out on which day of the moon phase you were born. Perhaps you would find it more interesting to check the next generation to see whether the gypsy rules are correct. You may succeed, to your surprise. If a baby is born in the next year, you only have to check a moon calendar and count a little bit, and you will have the first prophecy for the baby's future life. Don't worry, this is gypsy wisdom and will only predict good fortune.

If Your Next Birthday Falls on a New Moon... A Prognosis for the Next Year

The most certain prediction that we can make about our future is that it will surprise us.

Leonard

This wisdom may be common knowledge, but it has not prevented humanity from trying again and again for thousands of years. The oldest pipe dreams of men seek to know what the future might bring. There were and still are methods to predict the future—from the reading of entrails, to penny arcade fortune tellers, to astrology. These can all claim a certain percentage of correct hits. Only a few serious astrologers claim these days that they can precisely predict certain events. This does not mean that they won't strive to do so, within certain limits. Most of them, however, are content with general warnings and vague hints about future developments that can be observed from a natal chart. Even renowned British astrologers Derek and Julia Parker have looked into the oracle of the moon. Their prognosis regarding your fate in the following year, if your birthday falls into one of the major moon phases, is as follows.

New Moon

If your birthday falls on the new moon, the following twelve months can be an important time for you. It is possible that changes will occur that will influence your whole life. Often, these concern your attitudes and feelings. Perhaps you will meet a new partner, end an existing relationship, raise a family, or move. No matter what, the next year is the right time for new developments.

Full Moon

If your birthday falls on the full moon, a year rich with events lies before you. There will be changes, which will bring the best for you. Control your impulsiveness and unpredictability and follow your intuition, but do not trust it blindly.

Lunar Eclipse

A lunar eclipse can only occur at the full moon. The sun lights up the earth; the earth then casts a shadow across the universe. When the full moon moves into this shadow, a lunar eclipse takes place. A total eclipse occurs when the moon moves completely into the earth's shadow. If the shadow only partially hits the moon, a partial lunar eclipse occurs. Such an episode can last for several hours.

In former times, when nobody knew how a lunar eclipse happened, it was the cause of fear and horror. For thousands of years, it was considered to be an omen of catastrophe. Astrologers shared this belief, predicting death and disaster during such an eclipse. Have no fear; because we now know how an eclipse happens, it has lost its horror. Modern astrology speaks of enhancing the general influence of the unpredictable full moon. A lunar eclipse appears only about two times a year. If this event falls on your birthday, the following twelve months may be a keynote in your life. Do not scatter your energy. Focus on what is really important. Do not act merely on your feelings, but listen to good advice.

The above maxims apply to anyone, no matter in which phase his birthday falls. You cannot go wrong if you follow them!

Table 14

Lunar Eclipses 1996 to 2001

1996	April 4, September 27
1997	March 24, September 16
1998	March 13, August 8, September 6
1999	January 31, July 28
2000	January 21, July 16
2001	January 9, July 5, December 30

Did you know?

Columbus and the Lunar Eclipse

The world has many myths and legends about lunar eclipses. Nearly all of them are highly dramatic. The Chinese, for example, were convinced that hungry dragons devoured the moon. In many civilizations, the custom was to shoo away with much shouting and noise the dragons, evil spirits, and monsters that threatened the moon. As astrologers learned more about the earth-sun-moon relationship, it became possible to predict such phenomenon. Then the darkness lost its horror.

Christopher Columbus was an ingenious discoverer and a good astronomer, but not always a sterling character. He used his knowledge in the following way. In 1504, he landed on the shores of Jamaica. The inhabitants were reluctant to supply food to him and his crew. Columbus knew that a lunar eclipse would occur shortly. If they did not give them food, he threatened, the moon would change color and lose its light. When this actually happened, the natives became so frightened that they gave him more than food; they elevated him to godhood. One never knows!

The Moon in Everyday Life

It is certainly helpful to know the condition of one's own emotions. Knowing your moon sign can help you be more aware of your basic emotional patterns. In daily life, knowing which sign and which phase the moon is in can help you better understand and more easily master crises and times of "normal lunacy." The moon influences the many little details that can have an unconscious effect on the ups and downs of business. As we make important decisions, we as well as those around us are often under the sway of the moon's position.

Why is it that one day a party is a big success, and on another day it does not work, even though the same people are there? Why are you full of confidence and determination when you face your boss one day, and on another day you do not dare look him in the eye, much less discuss with him the long-due raise in salary? Of course, there may be a thousand good reasons. Today, we tend to blame everything on the weather. When we are moody, without impetus, or aggressive, it must be the weather. When a loved one snaps because he cannot find the cap of a toothpaste tube, when everybody cuts ahead of you on the way to work, when the waiter in the restaurant slams the plate on the table at lunch time—it is all because of a Santa Ana or a Sirocco wind.

Is it really such an absurd idea to think that the moon's position could cause some crises? If you are still skeptical, read about how the moon influences moods in the Chapter "The Moon and Madness" on page 145. In former times, people took for granted that the moon guided the wheel of daily life. This did not mean they checked the sky or the moon calendar each time they attempted a new venture. They probably accepted the lunar influence as part of their natural and intuitive contact with the rhythms of life.

We lost this sense a long time ago. Most of us have never looked at a moon calendar, or have not done so for years. These days, who knows where the moon is without looking into the sky or at a moon calendar?

Try to be a little more sensitive again. To know whether the moon is waxing or waning, a glance into the sky is sufficient. If this is too troublesome, you can get a watch that displays the moon phase each day. However, if you want to know which sign the moon is in, you have to look it up in a moon calendar (or see Table 17 on page 275 in this book).

There are no bad moon signs; there are only more or less favorable possibilities. Some days (for example, two to three days each month while the moon is in Pisces) are not favorable for tangible results. This does not mean that these are lost days. If you know when you will hit a Pisces day, you can at least prepare for it. Reflection, meditation, and inner relaxation are good activities for such days. Do not be afraid; you will not fall into lethargy. The next Aries day with its unharnessed energy is already knocking at the door.

There are two ways to find out about the moon's influence on daily life: the moon phases and the signs of the zodiac. The fastest and most comprehensive way is to consider the four main moon phases. Here again, we use the same system based on the law of lunar sympathy:

- waxing moon = increasing energy and strength
- waning moon = gradually decreasing energy, relaxation, and creative pause

The Moon Phases and Their Meaning in Everyday Life

Each of the four moon phases corresponds to a certain life rhythm. The yearly cycle from spring to winter, or a human life from childhood to old age.

First Quarter:

New Moon to Waxing Quarter Moon

The waxing new moon stands for the spring. It gives fresh energy. At long last, we pull ourselves up to start things that we have been putting off for a long time. We develop new ideas in our careers. In our private lives, we plan long overdue discussions to talk things out, the long-promised family trip, and spring cleaning. At the new moon and in the following first quarter, we write more letters (the mail man knows about this) and we make more phone calls (the operator can confirm this with a sigh) than on other days of the month.

Second Quarter:

Waxing Half Moon to Full Moon

This phase corresponds to the summer in the annual cycle. In the second quarter, most families feel a charged atmosphere, which reaches a critical level two days before the full moon. In the city, the traffic is terrible during rush hour. Colleagues at the office react more irritably. In many households, family disputes are in the air. Where there are crowds of people, mass hysteria can occur. In bars and pubs, the patrons drink more and there are more fights than at other times. This is a constantly repeated pattern that anyone can observe. Only scientists do not want to know about it, according to the maxim: "That which should not be, cannot be." Of course, being aware of the moon's influence does not mean that one can control it. At least one can try to remain quiet and serene during the emotional streak, and thus take the sting out of many situations.

Third Quarter:

Full Moon to Waning Half Moon

In the rhythm of the year, this phase corresponds to autumn. Only a few fresh starts are undertaken during this time. The third quarter is the time to ripen what was begun with enthusiasm during the first quarter. All one's energy should go into making a good finish for these projects. Parties planned during the first quarter are now celebrated and plans made in that phase are either put into action or rejected. Relationships and contacts that began in the first quarter are lived out. The third quarter is harvest time!

Fourth Quarter:

Waning Half Moon to New Moon

The fourth quarter is calmness before action, the gathering of energy before the new beginning. Nothing new starts now. This quarter corresponds to winter. It is time to withdraw for a while. Tranquillity, regeneration, and reflection are all timely. The next spring, brimful of energy, will surely come with the next new moon.

Rule of Thumb:

The Influence of the Four Moon Phases

- First Quarter: sprouting, reemergence, outwardly directed energy, reviving.
- Second Quarter: growth, development, shaping things that already exist.
- Third Quarter: maturing, bearing fruit, abundance, everything finds its final form.
- Fourth Quarter: dissolving, retiring, peace, reflection, pause before a new beginning.

First I must say: the sign through which the moon transits usually does not have enough influence to move mountains. This is because the moon moves much too swiftly. Although the moon plays an important role in one's personal horoscope, the moon transits usually pass without any remarkable outer influence. However, they do strongly influence the subconscious mind, and thereby unnoticeably influence one's actions. This is often evident in mood changes, fleeting encounters, and passing feelings. Even though one might not realize it, others sense it.

The influences that relate to each sign are as follows:

Moon in Aries

On these days, people feel more of a need to contact each other. They like to be in groups and to leap into activity with confidence. This enthusiasm, however, does not last long.

Moon in Taurus

This is a bad time for changes, especially in the financial area. Solid, conservative Taurus does not risk anything. However, any decisions that are made will be lasting, so be careful! Be especially wary of any spontaneous choices. Actions taken now will last for a long time and will be difficult to reverse.

Moon in Gemini

This is a changeable, hectic time. It is a good time for talking, negotiating, and exchanging ideas. Postpone action until later. It is also a good time for family gatherings and for meetings of a nonbinding nature.

Moon in Cancer

Here the moon is in its own sign. Thus, feelings and sensitivity are natural. People draw closer together, but beware of treading on someone's toes. During this time, many people are overly sensitive. Those who are easily influenced have to be especially cautious. Out of moodiness, one may eat more than is healthy.

Moon in Leo

Conversation, fun, and zest for life are the keynotes. Everybody gets up on stage and sells himself as best he can. This sign also supports the protective instincts and the need to care for the weak. Caution! Feeling possessive of someone will harm the relationship.

Moon in Virgo

This is not an easy time. The moon's need for contact is not harmonious with the self-denial and renunciation that are characteristic of this sign. This is a good phase, however, for details, organization, concentration, routine, and duty. It is also a good time for special offers and health regimes, and a bad time for independent and creative ventures.

Moon in Libra

This is a good period for romance, friendship, and partnership. Take time for yourself and avoid emotional conflict. There is a danger of reacting with jealousy and possessiveness, and you may find it difficult to be objective and distant.

Moon in Scorpio

Critical and superstitious behavior, especially pertaining to money are characteristic of this phase. Increased sensitivity and vulnerability can lead to a crisis. People tend to focus on habits and rituals. People with ESP can expect their faculties to be stronger.

Moon in Sagittarius

The longing to be free of a plodding routine is strong during this phase. Many people suffer from inexplicable restlessness, and try to escape from the habitual. This is a good time to contact people from foreign countries.

Moon in Capricorn

Career and business are in the foreground. These are the days of tradition, authority, and discipline. There is also a tendency toward pessimism, frustration, and depression.

Moon in Aquarius

These are the days of social engagements and rational thinking. It is a good time for new ideas and planning for the future. Anyone who is too idealistic should anticipate disappointment. Women often step into the foreground of a group, family, or circle of friends.

Moon in Pisces

This is a good time to be alone. It is ideal for pondering the spiritual and the mystical. Many people are unsociable at this time. They keep their emotions to themselves. There is a general feeling of insecurity and lack of confidence.

And now, after all the theory—practice. If you are in doubt about any projects you are contemplating, consult the following table that shows the moon signs for a variety of activities. However, please do not do as the Romans did. Ammianus Marcellinus described conditions in the fourth century A.D., after Emperor Constantine officially converted to Christianity. Even 1500 years later one senses his disapproval: "Many people neither bathe nor eat nor appear in public unless they have thoroughly checked Mercury's position and aspects to the moon according to the rules of astrology. It is strange that this naive belief can be found in those who question the heavenly forces."

Table 15

Moon Rules for Every Day
The Best Days to Do Anything

Activity	*Moon sign*	*Moon phase*
Advertising	Aries, Taurus, Gemini, Leo, Libra, Scorpio, Sagittarius, Aquarius	
Air travel	Sagittarius	
Airing beds	Aries, Leo, Sagittarius, Gemini, Aquarius, Libra	3 - 4
Art exhibition, Gallery, Museum	Libra	
Arts and crafts (sewing & handicrafts)	Taurus, Gemini, Cancer, Virgo, Libra, Capricorn	
Beautifying the home	Cancer, Libra	
Bicycle trip	Gemini	
Budgeting	Taurus, Cancer, Scorpio, Capricorn	
Business	Aries, Cancer, Libra, Capricorn	1 - 2
Business trip	Sagittarius	
Business, Long term	Capricorn	
Car repair	Taurus, Leo, Scorpio, Aquarius	3 - 4
Church visit	Pisces	
Conferences	Libra, Sagittarius, Capricorn, Aquarius	
Cooking	Taurus, Cancer, Leo, Aquarius	

Activity	*Moon sign*	*Moon phase*
Creative activities (painting, writing)	Gemini, Aquarius, Pisces	
Cultivate friendship	Gemini, Cancer, Leo, Libra, Sagittarius, Aquarius, Pisces	
Cultivating relationships	Gemini, Libra, Sagittarius	
Dance, Party	Leo, Libra	
Dancing	Gemini, Leo, Aquarius	
Dining out	Taurus, Cancer	
Dinner party	Taurus, Cancer, Leo	
Diving	Pisces	
End a relationship, with least hurt	Gemini	4
Enhancing education	Sagittarius, Capricorn	
Enjoying art	Libra	
Esoteric matters	Pisces	
Family visit	Taurus, Cancer, Libra, Leo, Capricorn	
Gambling	Capricorn, Aquarius	
Giving lectures	Sagittarius, Capricorn	1 - 2
Hobby collecting	Cancer	
Horse races	Sagittarius	
House painting	Taurus, Leo, Scorpio, Aquarius	3 - 4

Activity	*Moon sign*	*Moon phase*
Household affairs	Taurus, Cancer, Virgo, Libra, Capricorn	
Interviewing for a job	Leo, Sagittarius	1
Investing money	Taurus, Cancer, Scorpio, Capricorn	1 - 2
Laundry (soil comes out easier)		3 - 4
Legal appointments	Libra, Sagittarius	1 - 2
Loans	Capricorn	
Luxury	Leo, Libra	
Make out a will	Taurus, Leo, Scorpio, Aquarius	1 - 2
Meditation	Taurus, Scorpio, Capricorn, Pisces	
Money affairs	Aries, Cancer, Libra, Capricorn	
Movies	Leo, Aquarius	
Moving	Taurus, Leo, Scorpio, Aquarius	
Music playing & listening	Taurus, Cancer, Leo, Scorpio, Aquarius, Pisces	
Negotiating	Gemini, Cancer, Libra, Capricorn	
New job	Taurus, Virgo, Capricorn	
Ocean	Cancer, Scorpio, Pisces	
Open savings account	Taurus	1 - 2

Activity	*Moon sign*	*Moon phase*
Parties	Taurus, Gemini, Leo, Sagittarius, Aquarius	
Phone calls, long	Gemini	
Picnic	Aries, Leo, Sagittarius	
Planning & Organizing	Virgo, Scorpio, Sagittarius, Capricorn	
Political reading	Leo, Aquarius	
Psychotherapy	Scorpio	
Purchase car	Taurus, Leo, Scorpio, Aquarius (fixed)	
Quest for knowledge	Pisces	
Reading	Gemini	
Rebellion, Protest	Aquarius	
Relaxation	Taurus, Cancer, Leo, Libra, Pisces	
Repair of appliances	Aquarius, Virgo	
Repairs, simple jobs	Virgo	
Romance	Cancer	
Sales	Aries, Taurus, Gemini, Cancer, Leo, Libra, Sagittarius, Capricorn	
Seminars & Extension courses	Sagittarius, Capricorn	
Sex & Flirtation	Aries, Taurus, Leo, Scorpio, Sagittarius, Aquarius	
Shopping	Leo, Libra	

Activity	*Moon sign*	*Moon phase*
Shopping in health food stores	Virgo, Scorpio	
Social gathering	Gemini	
Sports	Aries, Gemini, Leo, Sagittarius, Capricorn	
Sports event, competition	Sagittarius	
Start building	Taurus, Leo, Capricorn, Aquarius	
Studying for exam	Virgo, Scorpio, Sagittarius, Capricorn, Aquarius	
Swimming	Cancer, Pisces	
Taking Pictures	Leo, Pisces	
Theater, Concert	Leo, Sagittarius	
Travel	Aries, Gemini, Sagittarius, Aquarius	
Trip	Gemini, Sagittarius, Capricorn, Aquarius	
Trip to the country	Aries, Taurus, Virgo, Sagittarius, Aquarius, Pisces	
Trip to the sea	Cancer, Pisces, Taurus, Leo, Scorpio	
Visit grandparents	Cancer	
Visit museum	Libra, Sagittarius	
Weaning	Sagittarius, Aquarius, Pisces	

Activity	*Moon sign*	*Moon phase*
Wedding	Taurus, Cancer, Leo, Aquarius	
Writing	Gemini	
Writing letters	Gemini, Virgo, Sagittarius, Pisces	

If no moon sign or phase is listed with an activity, then it does not play an important role.

Part IV

The Moon and Magic

The Moon and Witches

Take spawn of frogs and tongues of toads, mix well,
distill this carefully in full-moon light;
apply, where needed only, as the moon is waning,
and when spring comes your spots will all be gone.

Mephisto's freckle recipe from Goethe's Faust, Part II

Since ancient times, the moon and magic have belonged together. How else can it be? The moon rules the night—the world of the dark, the obscure, the hidden. Many figures of the night are in some way also part of the magical world. Everyone knows that ghosts and vampires always appear around midnight, preferably at the full moon. Harmless people change into raging werewolves only when the full moon is shining. The night is also the time for witches and magicians, whose goddess is the moon. They get their magic power from the moon, which they worship as the triune goddess: the trinity of Artemis (the waxing moon), Selene (the full moon), and Hecate (the waning and new moon). At the full moon, this power is strongest. Thus, witches' covens nearly always take place at the full moon. Even today this is so. The Wiccans still call their members together on full moon nights. Today, as in the olden days, their gathering opens with an invocation to the great goddess, from whom the Wiccans ask fertility, feminine power, and renewal.

Dancing around a fire is an ancient magical activity. When witches danced around a fire, they always looked into the flames and smoke. In this way, they absorbed the power of the special herbs and wood they had thrown onto the embers. They derived similar powers when they spent full moon nights outdoors looking at the moon. These nocturnal excursions have always been regarded with suspicion by other people. According to farm gossip, witches and wise women did not travel through the woods in the moonlight simply to gather useful plants and roots. The peasants thought this was only an excuse. In reality, the witches supposedly spent the night outdoors to be undisturbed while they called on wood goblins, stars, and planets, and especially the moon. Through invoking these, the witches gained enough magic powers to last until the next full moon. When they stared at people, witches could use their power to confer positive and negative qualities.

The peasants especially feared the waning moon, primarily the dark nights before the new moon. During this time when the moon shows its dark side, it was said, the time of the dark arts begins. Magic has only had a negative reputation since the Middle Ages, however. Before that, witches, wise women, magicians, healers, and midwives (who also had magical abilities) were considered normal people. Only those dark figures who specialized in black magic were regarded with terror. Increasingly impatient and hungry for power, the church eradicated (in the name of the merciful God) all who might threaten their might. Harmless midwives, healers, village magicians, and wise women were accused of being handymen of the devil. Millions were killed, victims of superstition.

Magic Rituals

Magic rituals have remained practically unchanged since ancient times, handed down in occult books called *Grimoires*. In the sixteenth and seventeenth centuries, the Grimoires were very popular. Many magic handbooks remain from these times, claiming to be very old—which seems to be true in most cases. The oldest is Solomon's Key, named after the wise king of the Old Testament, to whom God allegedly gave—besides wisdom—dominion over the hosts of demons.

Not only rituals but also the applications of magic have remained unchanged for thousands of years. The main intention has always been to gain power over souls, either by doing good for someone, seducing him by love spells, averting damage (generally known as white magic), or causing misfortune to befall an enemy. Of course, this last is black magic.

So that magic would succeed, highly complicated rituals were necessary. Each gesture had a precise meaning. While uttering a

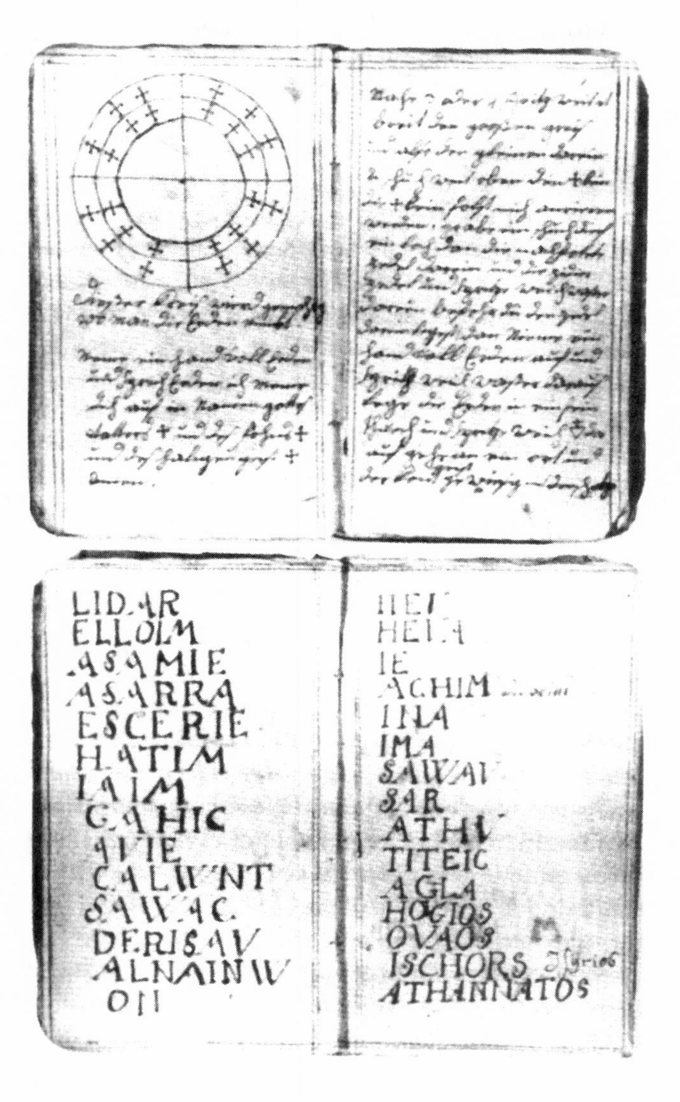

Illustration 9:
A Small Spell Book, 18th Century

simple curse, a witch had to whisper the victim's name three times and point the middle and index finger of the left hand. These two fingers allegedly represented the moon horns. The index finger represented Jupiter, the middle finger Saturn; together, they signified fortune and misfortune, building and destroying. A witch always possessed both potentials. People in Mediterranean countries still use this gesture with pointed fingers as an obscenity, but with a different meaning. When someone makes the horns, and perhaps says the swear word *cornuto* ("cuckold"), he is telling an adversary that his wife has betrayed him.

The Evil Eye

For a certain kind of magic, no words, gestures, or magic herbs were necessary. The evil eye was sufficient to destroy humans and animals. In the olden days, the evil eye was believed to be widespread. Not only did witches have it, but many other people whom one would never suspect also had it. In the sixteenth and seventeenth centuries, elderly women were highly suspect. Men and women born under a certain sign of the zodiac also belonged to this group (which sign, I unfortunately could not find out). Such dangerous villains would stare at little children or the animals in a stall. Then, according to the superstition, they just wasted away. For this reason, people veiled cradles and blindfolded animals. Anxious and endangered people wore amulets that symbolized the moon to protect themselves against the evil eye. Nearly all gypsy maidens of former times wore a necklace of silver and gold. According to old astrological ideas, these metals were related to the moon (silver) and sun (gold).

By the way, the ancient Egyptians were afraid of the evil eye and had an effective spell against it. They protected themselves, their belongings, their houses, and even their graves with the symbol *udjatti*, which depicted two eyes. The right eye symbolized the sun; the left, the moon. Together, the Egyptians believed, they were powerful enough to resist the evil eye.

Illustration 10:
The ancient Egyptian udjatti protected one from the evil eye.

Voodoo Dolls and Toggelis

Most magic will work only with the appropriate incantation. There are plenty of such magic formulas. The *Grimoires* contained magic formulas for every purpose. Rituals often enhanced the effect of this verbal magic. In former times, these were mysterious, but nowadays their principles are easy to see through. Mostly, they use analogy magic and contact magic, or a mixture of both. Analogy magic is a miniature imitation of the desired event. For example, if one wants to attract rain, the magic action would be to pour water on a hot stone accompanied by certain ceremonies. In so-called contact magic, the spell caster enchants a small fragment from the body of the victim (e.g., hair or fingernails) as a proxy for that person.

Today, some people still practice such rituals as voodoo in South America and Africa. Voodoo has been known in Europe since the Middle Ages. Magic specialist Sergius Golowin says in his book *The Wise Women* that the most feared curse in Switzerland, besides the evil eye, was the making of so-called witch dolls (*Atzmänner*, or more fondly *Toggelis*).

In the United States, they are known as *kitchen witches*. Such a Toggeli was sewn from the victim's old clothing, or the victim was portrayed as accurately as possible in wax or clay. The most important ingredient was to fix the real fingernails or hair of the victim on the doll. These dolls were made in the moonlight and were kept for one month. They were carried, usually by the light of the full moon, to a place that was important either to the victim or the witch. Needles, preferably made of silver (the moon metal) or iron (Mars), were held up to the sky three times so that they sparkled in the moonlight and were then stuck into the part of the Toggeli that was supposed to be harmed on the enemy (or even to destroy him). A horrible revenge would be to destroy the reproductive ability of a man or the fertility of a woman by stabbing the Toggelis in the groin area at the waning moon!

Diabole

This is a powerful magic handed down from the ancient Greeks. They used diabole in order to literally catapult their enemies to the moon. Exactly how they accomplished this has unfortunately not been passed down to us. We only know that, instructed by their customers, sorcerers told the moon what kind of evil the victim had done. Then the sorcerers asked for the offender's punishment. This may not have been as easy as it sounds. Something was certainly added to the magic, but nobody ever recorded it. We only know that the diabole must have been extremely effective. A magician named Pachrates was the court magician of the Roman emperor Hadrian. He was so successful that his enthusiastic employer doubled his salary! This was probably not a selfless act; according to the legend, by means of a diabole, Pachrates could bring a person from wherever he was to the emperor's court within one hour if the emperor commanded it. He could make an enemy sick within two hours. In order to kill him, Pachrates needed seven hours.

Moon Magic

Besides the usual magic (in which the moon often played a major role), a special moon magic was practiced in the West. The first requirement was to attract the moon's attention, which seems to have been difficult. The moon must have behaved like a real diva. The correct lunar position for the intended magic was the most important factor.

The waning moon was reputedly the optimal time for curses. This time was also good for studying ancient magic scriptures and for banishing negative energies. The dark nights immediately before the new moon were for performing the worst magic. The new moon night itself was taboo for any type of magic. On this night, the sun and moon are conjunct (i.e., in the same house). Thus, one did not know whether a curse might have an unpleasant boomerang effect on the well-being of the enemy, or if it would have a disadvantageous effect on the magician. A waxing moon was always the time for white magic rituals to increase health, prosperity, and luck. The full moon, when magic power reached its peak, was the time to practice the most important enchantments.

The sign of the moon's position was also important. Magicians and witches paid attention to the movement of the moon through the zodiac, where it stays for about two to three days in each sign. Each lunar sign had its own meaning, which was considered when choosing the appropriate time for a spell. The different signs are good for the following.

Moon in Aries	protection and courage
Moon in Taurus	peace, growth, money
Moon in Gemini	study of old scriptures, prophecy, wishes
Moon in Cancer	love, family, emotions
Moon in Leo	sex, passion
Moon in Virgo	healing
Moon in Libra	partnership, relationship, marriage
Moon in Scorpio	self defense, courage, exorcism
Moon in Sagittarius	travel
Moon in Capricorn	exile and banishment
Moon in Aquarius	mysteries, secrets
Moon in Pisces	expanding consciousness, dreams, magic

Today, such moon magic might sound complicated. In those days, however, these were mere trifles; even magicians' apprentices could perform them in their sleep. It became more complicated when one had to choose the appropriate planet and the ideal time for each spell. Thank heavens that ancient magicians had a memory aid! Each of the seven planets known in those days had its own day of the week. Each planet reputedly had extreme magical potency on its special day.

Today, one still knows which planet was dedicated to which god. The French and Italian names are of more help than the German and English. The names of the Norse gods have also infiltrated our calendar. For example, Thursday is for Thor the god of thunder (Jupiter of the Romans) and Friday for Freia (Venus of the Romans).

Monday	Moon (English—Monday, French—lundi, Italian—lunedi)
Tuesday	Mars (French—mardi, Italian—martedi)
Wednesday	Mercury (French—mercredi, Italian—mercoledi)
Thursday	Jupiter (French—jeudi, Italian—giovedi)
Friday	Venus (French—vendredi, Italian—venerdi)
Saturday	Saturn (English—Saturday, German—Samstag)
Sunday	Sun (English—Sunday, German—Sonntag)

Finally, time played a role. Usually, this was not exact time as we know it today, but rather an ideal time based on the day beginning with sunrise and ending with sunset. The time span is calculated, according to the season, and divided by twelve. Thus, one gets the twelve hours of the day. It is not important if there are a few leftover minutes. To be exactly on the minute is not required. When the sun rises around 7:00 A.M. and sets around 7:00 P.M., the first hour is approximately from 7:00 to 8:00. Every day, the planet of the day rules the first hour after sunrise. On Monday, the first hour of the day is the moon hour, and the third and the tenth hours of the night are the same. Is this too complicated? Here it is easier:

The Magic Hours After Sunrise

Sunday:	4, 11
Monday:	1, 8
Tuesday:	5, 12
Wednesday:	2, 9
Thursday:	6
Friday:	3, 10
Saturday:	7

The Magic Hours After Sunset

Sunday:	6
Monday:	3, 10
Tuesday:	7
Wednesday:	4, 11
Thursday:	1, 8
Friday:	5, 12
Saturday:	2, 9

After the best hour was decided, the next step was to follow the ritual, including ritual cleansing, exactly calculated magic circles, required clothing, and the appropriate magical accessories. For specific moon spells, a magic wand had to be carved, preferably from a willow branch (which was astrologically assigned to the moon). Only an innocent child could cut the wand, or a man who walked backwards and grasped the branch between his legs. A burnt offering, preferably of dried leaves from a laurel or myrtle tree, was made to the moon goddess to enhance the effect of the ritual. The smoke established a harmonious relationship with the ruler planet, and blessed the magic tools, which were usually a silver chalice and a moonstone.

Aside from specific plant magic, the high magic rituals, which were the most effective, were so complicated that only a few specialists knew them. These were witches and magicians who had dedicated their lives to the study of magic and esoteric knowledge. They charged accordingly high prices for their services.

Those who could not afford the magic services of these experts had to rely on the available alternative, which was folklore. Folk

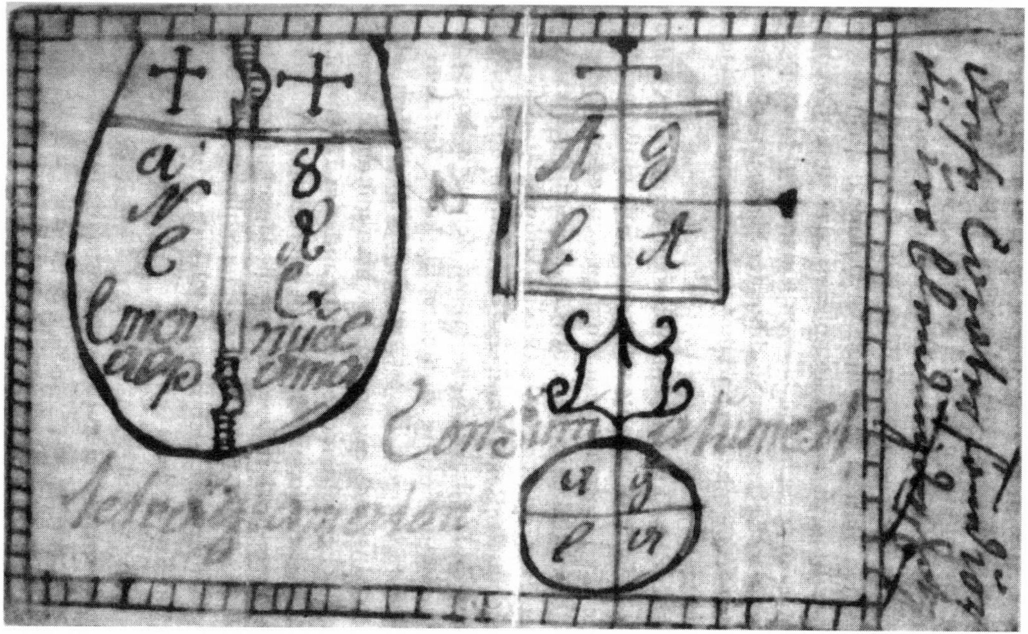

Illustration 11
Tablet with Magic Symbols

remedies and spells were simple forms of moon magic. Any village witch or wise woman could perform these magic formulas and rituals. However, even these women had an impressive knowledge of magic. For example, a village witch who took pride in her craft could make the moon disappear for at least a brief time. Unfortunately, we do not know whether or not she was able to do this trick only on nights of a lunar eclipse or on other nights as well.

Some people could not afford even the relatively humble—but still effective—witch magic lore. Those who found the services of a witch too expensive and too lavish could only find recourse in superstitions. These are still widespread. Here are a few examples.

Superstitions about the Moon

Good Luck Superstitions

- Seeing the sickle of the moon over the right shoulder is good luck.
- One who counts his money during the waxing moon increases it.
- Seeing the moon and at the same time touching a silver coin in your pocket brings good luck.
- Around Fronfasten (sixty days after Easter), a girl will see her future lover when she looks into a well near an alder tree.
- Store a sickle-shaped knife, called a witch knife, under a child's pillow. It will protect the child from witches' spells.
- New-Sunday and new-month day children are especially good at finding and rescuing hidden treasures. It was not easy to fulfill this requirement. A new-Sunday child must be born on a New Year's Day that was also a Sunday and a new moon day. A new month day child had to be born on the first Sunday of the month during a new moon period.

The following superstition carries the element of risk.

- Whoever sees the new moon sickle should, without talking, kiss the first person of the opposite gender who comes by. Then he will soon receive a present!

Bad Luck Superstitions

- Whoever sews during the moonlight sews his own shroud.
- Moonlight shining on the marriage bed will bring misfortune.
- Never spin in the moonlight; such yarn does not last. The spinner is also spinning the noose for her child.
- To dry laundry in the moonlight is to dry clothing that will have a connection with death.
- Bad luck will come to you if the full moon shines for the first time over your left shoulder.
- Never urinate while looking at the moon; it brings misfortune.

Do-It-Yourself Moon Magic

Fascinating or not, such a long list of special rules could easily discourage do-it-yourself magicians from learning more about moon magic. Fortunately, Scott Cunningham, a modern master magician and American bestselling author of magic books, sees a more pragmatic way. In his successful *Cunningham's Encyclopedia of Magical Herbs*, which he so humanly and unmagically dedicates to his mom and dad, he writes:

> *The ancients created magical systems with varying degrees of complexity. One area in which they excelled was the art of timing ritual acts in accordance with astronomical phenomena. Some of these systems were rigidly controlled by the phases of the moon; others took the seasons into account, and in yet others, the stars and their positions were all-important.*

Some of these systems are still in use today, with good results. But any system can kill spontaneity and hinder the effects of magic—even its very performance. Timing is important, true, but there should be only one inviolable rule: magic is used when needed.

If I have a headache that disturbs my sleep or work, I cannot wait for the moon to enter the proper sign, or until Ursa Major rises; I need relief immediately.

This is a trifling example, but it holds true for all magic. It is no use waiting three weeks to perform a money spell if your bills must be paid by the end of the week.

I am not arguing that timing with the planets, stars, seasons, lunar phases and so on does not provide extra power to spells: I am simply arguing against the necessity for such extra power. If the magic works, it will work at any time of the day or night.

I can hear ghostly complaints from magicians—'You can't perform love spells during the waning moon.' 'Money spells fail unless performed on a Thursday during spring while the moon is in Taurus, at the third or tenth hour of the night.'

Such pronouncements are common in magic—usually from people who do little or no practical work. Spells need not have ideal astronomical, seasonal, and weather conditions to be successful.

Those who wish to follow the old ways of timing magic with the sun, moon and stars can find this information in any good magical textbook, but it is by no means a necessity.

If you need courage before facing a job interview, don't look at the phase of the moon—grab some thyme and get on with it! [pp. 5-6]

Cunningham's Encyclopedia of Magical Herbs has some other interesting uses for thyme (thymus vulgaris). Placed under your pillow, it chases away nightmares and gives regenerating sleep. The scent of thyme will give you courage and energy.

Moon Magic for Beginners

In case you would like to try some moon magic on your own, here are a few simple rituals for amateurs. Most are love spells, because these have always been the most popular. "Will they work?" you may ask. Well, this might depend on how strongly you believe in their success. To find out why this is so important, read "Does Magic Really Work?" on page 252. If you are a beginner, it might be good to consider the correct lunar phase. After all, you never know.

Love Spell: French

If you want to know who your next lover will be, step outside at night while the moon is in its first quarter and say the following spell:

Mother Moon, let me see
The man (woman) who will go with me.

You must repeat this on seven nights. On the seventh night, you will see your future lover standing before you in a dream. At any rate, the old French book of spells containing this rhyme promises you will.

A Spell for Larger Breasts

In modern southern Italy, young girls and women who want larger bosoms continue to perform the following ritual.
During a waxing moon, stand completely nude on the balcony or roof of your house. Raise your hands in supplication to the moon goddess. Then touch your bosom and say nine times (nine is the magic moon number):

Santa Luna, Santa Stella,
Fammi crescere
Questa mamella.

Or in English:

Holy moon, holy star
Let this bosom
Grow for me.

> To ensure that the goddess will know which breasts to enlarge, you have to touch your bosom on the word *questa* (this). Also, do not mispronounce the rhyme during the nine repetitions, or the magic will have no effect.

Does this work? The American philologist who discovered this magic formula swears that he has never seen a small-chested Neapolitan woman.

Love Spell: Ancient Grecian

This is a spell for the advanced practitioner. It belonged to the treasure of the highly regarded ancient witch, Simaitha, and was passed down by Theocritus.

> To enchant the object of your affections, wind red wool yarn around a sacrificial vessel while invoking Selene, Artemis, and Hecate. Burn laurel, wheat flour, and a thread from the coat of your beloved in the vessel. Smear the ash of this sacrificial offering onto the threshold of the loved one and say:
>
> *I am grinding the bones of the dolphin.*
>
> Then spit.

Of course, doing this makes it higher magic! Simpler, but equally effective, is the following spell from England. It also has to do with the moon, and should be spoken during a new moon, which is especially good for love spells.

Love Spell: English

Look at the new moon over your right shoulder while saying:

New moon, new moon, tell me
Who my own true love will be
The color of his hair and the clothes that he will wear
And the happy day that he will wed me.

You will dream of your future husband the next night.

Love Spell Without Words

Lastly, a spell that you do not speak.

> Collect as many cherry pits as you are years old. Every night, pierce a hole through one of the pits. Start piercing on the night after the new moon, and stop when the moon starts to wane. This limits you to a maximum of fourteen pits per month. When you have pierced all the pits, wait for the next new moon. String the pits on a pink string and tie it around your left knee for fourteen nights. You can take it off during the daytime.

This spell is guaranteed to bring you the desired man or woman.

Herbal Teas With a Magical Effect

Perhaps you do not need any love spells at this time, and would prefer to experiment a little with magic herbs. For example, how would you like to try a certifiably safe herbal ritual? Besides healing, herbal teas also have a magical effect. However, only insiders know this.

> Carefully choose one of the following magic plants and brew a special tea from it. For one cup use about one teaspoonful of the herb. Pour boiling water over it, preferably pure spring wa-

ter. Cover while steeping. Light a candle and wait. While the tea is steeping, the magical effect of the herb passes into the drink.

Magic Herbs and Their Effects

Alfalfa	purification
Catnip	peace
Chamomile	love
Elderblossom	protection
Ginger	protection
Hibiscus	clairvoyance
Lemon balm	health
Lemon grass, Rose, and a little Cinnamon	clairvoyance
Licorice root	love and sex
Sage	longevity

Did you know?

Gypsy Magic

Gypsies have a great tradition of magic and superstition. Since ancient times, the moon has belonged among their deities. By the way, a legend about the moon goddess is responsible for the gypsies' wandering for all eternity. According to the myth, the sun god was once king of the gypsies. He tried to seduce his sister, the moon goddess, but she continually escaped him and is still escaping him.

The nomadic gypsies met regularly at every full moon, not only because of its power to support human fertility, but also because they could remember such a date without error. Also, the gypsies believed that God did not make this night especially bright and beautiful just so people could sleep through it! Great power allegedly pours down to the earth through the light of the moon. All plants have the highest sap, and prepared foods and drinks are especially juicy, tasty, and digestible. What an ideal time to celebrate!

The focus of the festivity was eating and drinking. Mostly, the gypsies ate strange dishes from Eastern countries. They were spiced with a lot of earth magic and the right plants from native woods. These recipes were thought to give life force, fertility, and procreation until an advanced age to the nomadic folk. Nobody felt tired the next morning. One who celebrated throughout the full moon night, the gypsies believed, would not be tired the next morning, but instead feel fresh and renewed.

Magic Plants

Magic formulas and moon rituals were, of course, only one side of magic. At least equal in importance were magic herbs.

Not only can plants heal or kill; they can also change consciousness in a magical way. This especially fascinated people in the Middle Ages and led to countless legends. Knowledge of the magical effects of plants was a closely guarded secret, only available to initiates. Thus, herbal experts were not only revered and respected but also feared and threatened. They led dangerous lives that often ended at the stake.

Herb magic made a clear distinction between magic herbs and witchcraft herbs. Magic herbs were beneficial. Their mere presence, whether kept in the house or worn on the body, could reputedly ward off all evil and bring health, luck, and wealth. Witchcraft (or devil's) herbs were harmful. No one but witches and magicians were allowed to handle them. In correct dosages, they caused euphoria and awakened supernatural powers. They were used in ointments, incense, and magic potions. Hallucinations, feeling able to fly, and intense lust could occur by ingesting them or rubbing them on the skin. We know which herbs had these effects. In the olden days, this was also probably common knowledge. However, the required means of selection, combination, and dosage to achieve the desired effects remained strictly secret. Because many witchcraft herbs were highly poisonous, experiments by laymen often ended in death. People were usually content to leave this knowledge to the herb witches.

Dangerous Witchcraft Herbs

The leaves and berries of the mandrake *(Mandragora officinarum)*, the most famous of all magic plants, were important in traditional magic as a means of altering consciousness. The root was cherished as a magic plant in the positive sense. See page 240 for a history of the mandrake.

Datura *(Datura stramonium)* was an ingredient in witches' ointments in the Middle Ages. It could enhance a man's potency and induce erotic dreams.

Hemlock *(Conium maculatum)* was the main ingredient in flying ointment. The alkaloid *coniine* in hemlock sap gives a sensation of flying when taken orally or rubbed into the skin.

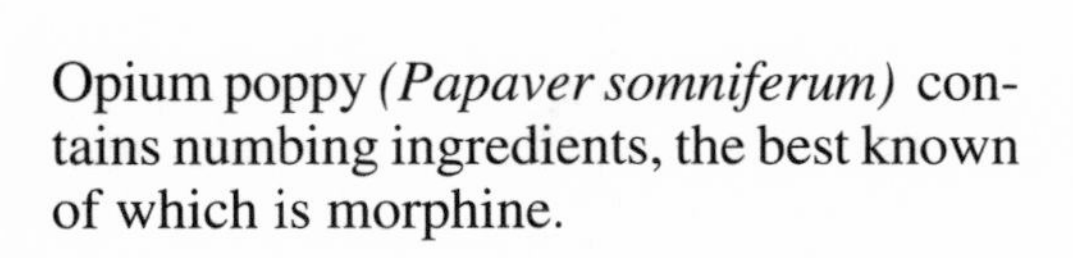

Opium poppy *(Papaver somniferum)* contains numbing ingredients, the best known of which is morphine.

Belladonna *(Atropa belladonna)* contains a substance that, when highly diluted, can allegedly enhance sexual excitement in women. Thus, it was an important ingredient in love potions and witches' ointments. Because belladonna enlarges the pupils, women who wanted to be more beautiful dropped a diluted extract into their eyes.

Henbane *(Hyoscyamus niger)* in the form of a potion was offered as a welcome drink at the witches' sabbath. Its strongly sedative effect supposedly took away new members' fears about facing their initiation rites.

Bittersweet nightshade *(Solanum dulcamara)* is a narcotic that was put into witches' ointments and incense.

Monks hood *(Aconitum)* had an ancient reputation as an extremely strong poison. In the olden days, those sentenced to die had to eat this tuber. It was also an ingredient of witches' ointments.

Since ancient times, herbs have been granted magical properties. Many plants were worn on the body as amulets or talismans, were put into beds, or were hidden in secret places in the house. Of course, it was always related to love. In order to achieve the desired effect—health, protection, a husband, or wealth—it was necessary to gather the plants according to a definite ritual. The more rare or precious the plant, the more complicated its picking ritual. The ritual used for the mandrake, the queen of magic herbs, was especially gruesome.

Mandrake *(Mandragora officinarum)* root was used as a vehicle for spells. Our ancestors assumed that its humanlike shape contained wondrous powers. Its magic root could allegedly answer every question one asked of it. It was able to predict the future, heal disease, bring wealth, help women at birth; in brief, it was priceless.

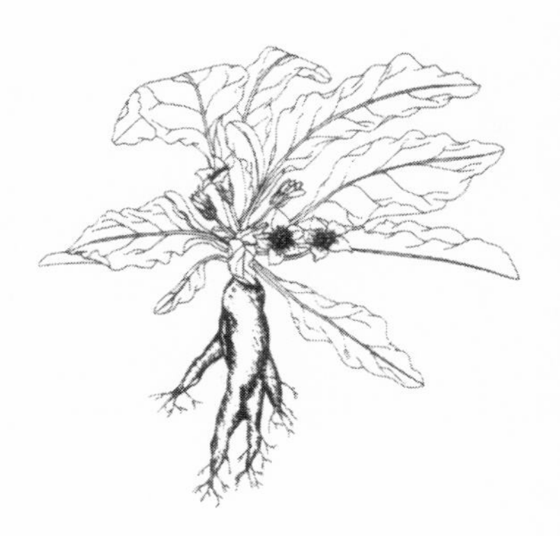

No wonder everyone who could afford it wanted to possess such a magic root. However, this was not easy; mandrake was as precious as it was rare. An herb book from the early Middle Ages explains why. According to the *Pseudo-Apuleius Herbarius*, mandrake possesses a nearly divine power and becomes invisible in the presence of any impure person. No wonder the mandrake business was full of swindlers! This flourishing business attracted countless fakes. The roots of many other plants such as bryony (Bryony alba) and Victoria's leek (Allium victorialis)—look similar to the mandrake. Swindlers risked severe punishment. Eventually the trade was officially forbidden; however, this only increased demand.

Someone lucky enough to find a true mandrake had to follow a specific ritual while digging the root. One could not pull it out of the soil without bringing about his own death. The book *Gottessegen der Kräuter* by Hilde Sieg graphically describes the process used in the Middle Ages for digging up a mandrake root:

> *On Friday before sunrise, a strong-hearted root-digger who wanted to win the magic powers of fortune went to the secret place where the plant grew. As a precaution, he plugged his ears with cotton or wax. He uncovered only the upper part of the plant, making a circular groove so that half the roots were still under the soil. To touch and pull up the plant would have caused his immediate death.*
> *For this purpose, he had a dog. This dog's fur had to be raven-black. It was starved for two days. The man carefully tied a rope around the mandrake, then tied it to the tail or neck of the dog. From a safe distance, he beckoned the dog with a piece off meat or bread. The dog pulled, and the mandrake uprooted itself with a heart-breaking moan and scream. The dog collapsed and died. He was the required victim.*
> *The gatherer carefully wrapped the little mandrake in white linen, and quickly brought it home, where he bathed it in red wine, dressed it in red and white silk clothing, and carefully handled it.*

Even nowadays, belief in the magic powers of this plant is not completely dead. In Cunningham's *Encyclopedia of Magical Herbs* (1992), modern magicians find the following instructions:

> *To 'activate' a dried mandrake root (i.e., to bring its powers out of hibernation), place it in some prominent location in the house and leave it there undisturbed for three days. Then place it in warm water and leave overnight. Afterwards, the root*

is activated and may be used in any magic practice. The water in which the root has bathed can be sprinkled at the windows and doors of the house to protect it, or onto people to purify them spiritually. [p. 148]

Mugwort *(Artemisia vulgaris)* is harmless compared to the mandrake. This ancient magic plant supposedly fended off disease and disaster, prevented exhaustion when tied to the feet of a hiker or traveler, and protected a house from lightning.

Vervain *(Verbena officinalis)* provided a rich harvest, chased away ghosts and spells, and could fend off storms.

Club moss *(Lycopodium clavatum)* was worn under clothing when someone had to appear in court. This would hopefully bring a favorable outcome to the legal proceedings. Nowadays, it is used for homeopathy. In order to avoid any negative influence on its characteristic effects, metal should not touch it. A golden sickle is used to harvest it, since gold is not only a neutral metal but also reputedly has healing properties. Harvesting club moss also means the acquisition of dark forces.

Did you know?

Plant Your Own Little Magical Love Garden

It does not have to be a mandrake. Perhaps you will fall in love for life—or longer—with this old recipe for a little love garden made with basil, lavender, and catnip.
When the moon is full, plant some lavender in the center of a clay flowerpot. Plant a circle of catnip around it. Plant a circle of basil around the catnip. If you want to be really sure that your love herbs have the desired effect, say the following spell while you are planting.

Plants of Venus
Under the full moon
Bring someone to me
Whom I can love.

Herbs That Chase Away Evil

These herbs are used to make the spells of evil ghosts, demons, and witches ineffective.

Hedge nettle *(Stachys recta)* was carried in one's pocket against the evil eye.

Elecampane *(Inula helenium)* was worn as an amulet on a cord around the neck. It was supposed to be protection against bewitchment, enabling one to fight the hexes of diseases such as lumbago and possession.

Valerian *(Valeriana officinalis)* was used to smoke out devils and witches. The same was true for arnica *(Arnica montana),* dill *(Anethum graveolens),* St. John's wort *(Hypericum perforatum),* tansy *(Tanacetum vulgare),* and wormwort *(Artemisia absin-thium).*

Garlic *(Allium sativum)* helped against the evil eye, and—as everyone knows—against vampires.

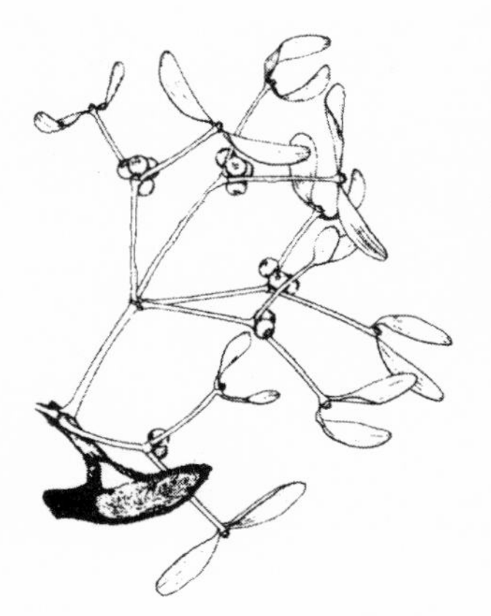

Mistletoe *(Phoradendron flaves-cens)* was effective against illness caused by hexes. It could also fight off evil spells, and much more.

Mistletoe and Moonlight

Most people today only know that mistletoe is an evergreen plant with white berries that one hangs indoors at Christmas. When a person steps under a mistletoe sprig, one can kiss him or her. The custom of this so-called kissing charm was originally common only in English-speaking countries. However, it has gained popularity in Europe in recent years.

When we cut or buy mistletoe, we honor a fertility ritual that was celebrated during the winter solstice (21 December) long before Christ. The founders of this ritual were probably the Celts, who inhabited large parts of Europe between 8,000 and 2,000 B.C. For a variety of reasons, mistletoe branches were sacred to them. It grew mostly as a parasite on oak trees, which were sacred to the Celts. To them, it seemed that the mistletoe appeared out of nowhere. Of course, today we know that it grew because its seeds were spread from bird droppings. However, the Celts had not figured this out. Only Druid priests were allowed to pick mistletoe. They observed strict ritual requirements. The harvest of mistletoe was in accordance with the lunar phase, as were many other sacred activities of the Celts.

Pliny the Elder described this sacred procedure very precisely in his book *Natural History.* On the sixth day after the new moon, the moon had exactly the right power. Then, a Druid mantled himself in white robes, climbed into an oak tree where mistletoe grew, and cut the branches with a golden sickle. Because the sprigs could not touch the earth, they were carefully caught in a white cloth. If by chance any mistletoe landed on the ground, it lost its magic effect. After the harvest, two white bulls were led to the oak tree and sacrificed there. Only after all this rigmarole were these holy branches used for fertility rites for man and animal. They were also a highly effective remedy against epilepsy and poisoning. Pliny compared the customs of the Celts with those of the Romans, and discovered many parallels regarding use, harvesting tools, and picking time. With respect to the moon, the Romans preferred the first and the Celts preferred the sixth day. Similar customs also existed in Zambia and Japan.

One can probably smile about the famous golden sickle, which every child has heard about since *Asterix* (a European comic strip that chronicles the ancient customs of the Germanic and Northern peoples). Gold is much too soft a metal for cutting. The Druids probably used gold-plated bronze or iron. However, we cannot overlook the sun-moon symbolism—gold stands for the sun, the sickle for the moon.

Herbs for Love Potions

Since ancient times, men and women have tried to enhance their attractiveness to members of the opposite sex. They used the following herbs, among others.

Lovage *(Levisticum officinale)* was mainly used by men.
Cuckoopint *(Arum maculatum)* was put into the shoes of young girls, while saying a rhyme, to make them attractive at dances.

European agrimony *(Agrimonia eupatoria)* was dug up with a non-iron tool on Good Friday. It brought a woman's love to a man. Chicory *(Cichorium intybus)* was used for the same purpose.

Healing Plants with Magical Effects

It was commonly believed that some plants could draw disease away from a person and take it into themselves. Of course, this procedure was not easy. Most of the time, a complicated ritual was required. Bistort *(Bistorta bistortoides)*, picked during a waning moon, allegedly worked against tumors. Cranesbill *(Geranium dissectum)* and knotgrass *(Polygonum aviculare)* could absorb eye and ear ailments if one knew the necessary rituals, which often involved the moon. For example, tuberculosis patients were pushed three times through a wreath of honeysuckle, which had been cut during a waxing moon in March, while ritual prayers were said. Burstwort (*Herniaria glabra*) supposedly helped heal hernias. One had to unearth it three days before a new moon and bind it in a poultice over the hernia for three successive nights. It remained there until the herb became warm. It was then cooled off and buried before the moon waxed. (Perhaps this simple way of taking medication is not so unappealing.)

Gathering Magic Herbs

All the old magic scriptures offered guidelines on when to collect the herbs used for magic. Plants could only fully develop their magic powers if they were collected at the proper time. Although different cultures sometimes had contradicting instructions, they did agree enough to give us a clear picture of the collection rituals for magic herbs. One nearly always collected the herbs before sunrise on a day of the week that was the ruler for the specific plant.

Monday	plants ruled by the Moon
Tuesday	plants ruled by Mars
Wednesday	plants ruled by Mercury
Thursday	plants ruled by Jupiter
Friday	plants ruled by Venus
Saturday	plants ruled by Saturn
Sunday	plants ruled by the Sun

The lunar phase was also important. Roots or wood had to be collected during a waning moon. Ancient magicians only picked blossoms, fruits, or seeds for magic purposes during a waxing moon. Some plants could only be picked on certain days (for example, May Day or Midsummer's Night).

Sometimes even the compass direction was important. That was when it started to get complicated. Agrippina described this in his work on occult philosophy. Facing west, one collected plants ruled by the moon, Venus, or Mercury. Facing south or east, one collected plants ruled by Mars, Saturn, and Jupiter. Facing south, one gathered sun plants.

Before acquiring these plants, the sorcerers had to take a bath, clothe themselves in white robes, and fast. They could not speak to anyone before setting out. Before cutting a plant, they sometimes made magic circles around the plant and dug it up with a nonmetal tool. Leaves, blossoms, roots, and seeds could under no circumstance touch the ground, or they would lose their magic effect (see mistletoe, above). Finally, the practitioners carefully bound the plants in a cloth and took them home. They used the plants fresh for especially strong magic effects, or dried them.

One could only collect particularly holy plants by means of certain rites. These requirements ranged from going barefoot (with washed feet) to harvesting only after offering wine and bread to the plant (as was the case with Selago, a species of juniper) to muttering incantations during the harvest process (while one washed the plants in mother's milk). Modern magicians and herbalists have different collection techniques. Because they feel responsible for the natural world, they only pick as much as they absolutely need, and always take care that enough seeds, blossoms, and leaves remain so that the plant can survive. However, they still observe the old rules of day, hour, and lunar phase. Sometimes they even follow the old tradition of offerings, but they always explain to the plant what they want to do, and why they have to pick or uproot it.

> ***Did you know?***
>
> *Fairy Rings*
>
> Fairy rings are circular tracks in the grass that catch the eye. Sometimes the grass has been trodden away, but at other times it may be remarkably thick. According to folklore, these rings originate from dancing fairies (or witches). An old legend said that if one circled around such a fairy ring nine times at midnight during the full moon, one could listen to the conversations of the fairies.

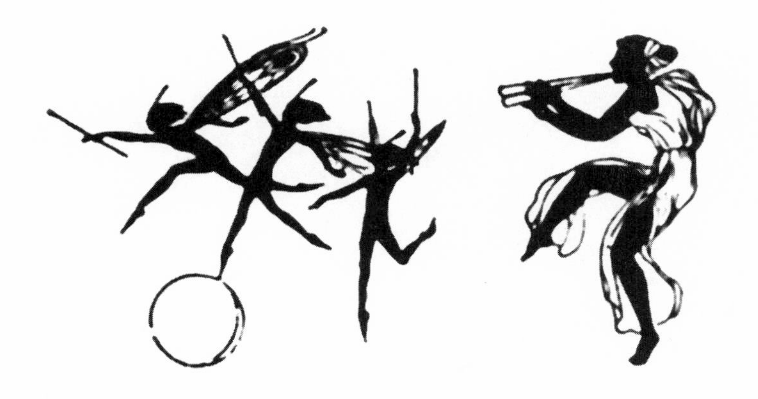

Illustration 12
Fairies Dancing with a Fairy Ring

What Ancient and Modern Magicians Attribute to the Moon

Activities	swimming, sailing, bathing, washing, cleansing, dreaming, daydreaming, nourishing, brewing
Animals	baboon, bat, beaver, cat, chameleon, hen, elephant, most fish, hare, sea turtle, sheep, shrimp, goose, crab, horse, otter, owl, panther, rabbit, sea lion
Astrological sign	Cancer
Body part	belly & breasts
Clothes	robes of silk or cotton, white dresses and hats, bathing suits, silver jewelry, necklaces, bracelets & bangles with moon symbols, white belts
Colors	white, silver, pastel
Drinks	milk, buttermilk, kefir, champagne, white wine
Food	coconut, eggs, fish, ice cream, shellfish, soups, vanilla pudding, yogurt, cream cheese recipes, white sauces
Fragrances	sandalwood, myrrh, rosewater
Fragrances for incense	1 part frankincense, 1/2 part sandalwood, 1/4 myrrh, 1/4 white rose petals, a pinch of poppy
Goddesses	Artemis, Diana, Selena, Persephone, Demeter, Hecate
Magical effect	love, peace, tranquillity, sleep, parapsychological consciousness, prophetic dreams, healing, beauty, fertility, birth
Magic tools	chalice

Moon phases and magic rituals	waxing moon for good spells, full moon for all kinds of spells, waning moon for curses & destroying negative energies
Musical instruments	gong, brass instruments
Musical note	B
Places	oceans, seas, creeks, rivers, lakes, springs, shores, wells, canals, waterfalls, restaurants, kitchens, homes, gardens, bathtubs, bedrooms, farms, boats that are at sea
Plants	camphor, cucumber, gardenia, jasmine, lemon, lemon balm, head lettuce, lily, lotus, myrrh, poppy, squash, sandalwood, sea grass, plants with white flowers, and those that bloom at night
Qualities	damp, fertile, nourishing, loving
Ruler of	family, mothers, children, tides, feelings, gardening, people born in Cancer
Season	autumn
Sense	taste
Stones	aquamarine, beryl, moonstone, selenite, quartz, rock crystal
Tarot cards	chalices
Weekday	Monday

Last but Not Least: Does Magic Really Work?

It remains to answer the question that everyone has probably already asked: Did magic really work in the olden days, or was it only imagination, illusion, charlatanry, and humbug? Also, if many of these writings are true, why does magic no longer work today? Perhaps it does still work? Our modern, critical attitude toward magic is only two hundred years old. Before that, everything that we consider hocus pocus was completely normal. Not just simple people, but everyone believed in it, including Martin Luther.

If we define magic as working with subtle energy to influence things, people, and situations on the soul level according to one's own ideas, then magic has always belonged to everyday life. Probably no era or civilization has been without it. Magic was routinely used to contact pagan deities and transcendent forces and thereby influence things in a desired direction. For thousands of years all over the world, magic rituals fended off disasters, sickened healthy people, and healed the sick. People indifferent to each other fell in love, and lovers became indifferent to each other.

These phenomena are all well documented, for instance in the legal records of witch trials. Although almost nobody knew how or why these spells worked, they were never doubted until the beginning of the scientific age. People did not even question magic's validity when a ritual occasionally failed. In those days, an unsuccessful magic ritual did as little to discredit magic as a defective television would to devalue technology today, or as a bungled surgery would jeopardize medicine. Besides, today we routinely handle another form of subtle energy, which does not relate to the soul, but rather is akin to the material level. It comes out of the electrical outlet and is called electricity. We all take it for granted as we use it, although this does not mean we really know what it is. For generations, scientists have strained their brains over this question. Without understanding the nature of the subtle energy known as electricity, we use it for television, computers, electric irons, and kitchen appliances. We think of this as completely normal. In reality, we handle a great mystery with matter-of-factness, just as in the olden days witches and magicians handled their soul-level magic.

There is a simple explanation why the old magic no longer functions in our modern world. To make magic effective requires an environment that English biologist Rupert Sheldrake calls a "morphic field" in his book *A New Science of Life*. A morphic field comes into being when the people of one culture perform a certain task again and again. The more often they perform this task, the easier it will become. In the euphoria over the seemingly unlimited possibilities of technology, magic has lost its importance. This weakens its morphic field and thus, proportionally, its effects.

However, we may now be at the dawn of a turnaround. We share the illusion that we have reached the peak of our development; all the generations before us also believed this but, until now, they were wrong. Meanwhile, it is increasingly apparent that our modern magic—technology—has pushed our world to the edge of disaster. It has definitely reached its limit. Future generations will belittle the technology of which we are so proud, just as we belittle the magic of the Middle Ages.

This does not mean that we have to slip back into the age of magic. However, we should not preclude the possibility that magic will play a greater role in our lives than it has during the past two hundred years. There are indications that this is so, which would mean that its morphic field is increasing and, thereby, its effectiveness, as well.

Did you know?

Faith Moves Not Only Mountains

Oxford graduate de la Warr discovered several decades ago that he could influence the growth of ailing or badly nourished plants in a positive way by directing ions toward them with a system of lenses that refracted the energy. After three years, he made a surprising discovery: man plays a much more important role in the procedure than does the instrument. The plants began to recover from their ailments from the moment he decided to radiate them. As if they had received a secret signal, they grew straight up. The scientist had only one explanation for this: The thoughts of a human being can influence the cell-building of the plant. The simple belief that some plants have to grow faster than others worked the miracle.

Did you know?

A Modern Wiccan Wedding

The modern Wiccans marry at the full moon. During the ceremony, a blue ribbon with a silver moon crescent is fastened in the bride's hair. A blue ribbon with a gold medallion symbolizing the sun is fastened in the groom's hair. When they "jump over the broom" together, they are declared man and wife. The full moon, and for some ceremonies the new moon, represents the highest energy. Wiccan followers say that if for Christians Sunday is the day when energy flows most strongly, for them, it is at the full moon.

Moon People and Their Qualities

In ancient astrology textbooks, we find primarily negative qualities for moon people. Supposedly, they are all snobbish, proud, vain, unsteady, anxious, good-for-nothing, provocateurs, born fools, and silly. One cannot avoid the impression that we have demonized the most feminine planet. Such demonization also occurred in ancient civilizations in Europe, and in the late Middle Ages.

This hostility was associated with an increasing disrespect for many ancient feminine professions. This antagonism peaked with the persecution of witchcraft. Although their professions were targeted, the real victims were women of knowledge and spirit. Ancient writers falsely accused them of worshipping the moon; superstition still perpetuates this belief today.

According to folklore, the moon rules over all the changes and transformations in nature. One can see this in many homilies about menstruation, pregnancy, the rising and falling of tides and sap in plants, and other such things. If this is so, then it must also be true that Luna (Diana) rules over people who are sensitive to these types of processes. Khalderasch gypsies claim that all modern wise women still invoke the moon for their work. These women are midwives; master herbalists for health, love, and fertility; and alternative physicians, who know how to work with the elements of water and earth.

When the moon shows its dark side, it is a model for people who seek to misuse their power. Then, natural feelings degenerate and intuition (or instinct) regarding black magic is aroused. Then it is possible to prepare poison to cause an abortion or to make other people sterile. The symbols for these depraved, corrupt "sciences" are the dark moon (the black circle) and the reversed moon horns (the bowl or the chalice pointing downward, indicating that all natural blessings stream out).

Excerpted from Bauer/Dümotz/Golowin: *Dictionary of Symbols*

Part V

The History of Moon Astrology

The Development of the Calendar

Since the existence of man, earth's inhabitants have observed the sky and tried to calculate time according to the planets. Of course, they only took into account what they could see with the naked eye. For thousands of years, our ancestors believed that earth was a flat disc, that the sky above was a dome, and that the stars stood fixed in it. When later Ionic philosophers discovered that the earth is a sphere, the theory followed that the sphere of the sky surrounded the sphere of the earth like a hollow ball. The sky turned around the planet once a day. The stars obviously did not move, but the sun and the moon traveled in regular cycles in their heavenly orbits. In the beginning, no one paid attention to the five extremely bright stars that regularly traversed the sky with apparent randomness.

The moon phases were easy to recognize. Thus, our ancestors probably discovered the lunar month as the first time unit after day and night. However, as pioneering as this discovery may have been, what people needed much more was a calendar of the seasons. They had to know when to sow, when the harvest would ripen, and when buffalo and gazelle herds would pass on annual migrations through their areas. They could only see this from the position of the sun. We may never know when humans succeeded in calculating the seasons from the orbit of the sun. At some point, they realized that the sun circles the earth in its heavenly orbit at different heights. Twice a year, when it reaches its highest point, it briefly pauses and then turns back. Either summer or winter begins once again. On two other days when it crosses the heavenly equator, daytime and nighttime boast equal length. The definitions of spring, summer, autumn, and winter came from these observations.

Lost in the darkness of history is the time when man began to use the fixed stars in the sky as reference points, and when the stars got their names. However, long before discovering the zodiac, our ancestors knew that spring begins when the sun is in Aries. When it moves into the sign of Gemini, it is the signal for shepherds to move to new pastures. When it sinks to Scorpio, it is the signal to close the fences for winter. Our ancestors also knew that the sun needs about 365 days to return to the spring equinox.

Compared with these complicated interrelationships, the cycle of the moon is child's play. In a continual rhythm, the first small crescent becomes full and round, then wanes, and eventually disappears for a few days, only to be reborn as a small crescent in the sky. There was no question for our ancestors that the sun and the moon were deities who wanted to give a message through their movements. The meaning of the sun was clear: it brought light, warmth, and the seasons. However, what did the moon want to tell them?

The Prehistoric Moon Calendar

In order to find this out, in prehistoric times, our ancestors had wrote down the orbit of the moon. Or, rather, they carved it in bone, rock, and ivory. Archeologists have found such moon calendars, which originate from between 40,000 and 8,000 B.C. They show a short line for a normal sunny day, and a long line for a full moon or new moon.

The cave paintings are equally old, but more precise. They have been discovered in Spain, among other places. In the center of the painting, you can find a moon deity resembling a human figure, surrounded by waxing and waning moon crescents, a thin line representing the new moon, and three dots representing the full moon and the day after the full moon. No error was possible. The time concept of a month was determined in the following way. The period from full moon to full moon or from new moon to new moon lasted for twenty-nine days and nights. Twelve lunar months—one lunar year—equaled about one solar year.

Soon it became obvious that the heavenly forces had given humanity a sign through this calendar. Knowledge of the rhythm of the sun and the moon was the first step in a tremendous developmental leap. Our ancestors developed agriculture around 10,000 B.C. They gathered wild grains and milled them between stones into a kind of flour. Then, the first tribes settled, building villages and systematically cultivating their grains. It became important to know the exact times for sowing and harvesting in order not to miss the right date in the next season. For example, wheat sown in June does not ripen until winter.

As generation after generation of our ancestors observed the sky, they realized that the moon was much more than a calendar. They discovered more and more interrelationships. For example, on warm summer nights, the full moon can cover meadows with dew, but never the new moon. A lunar eclipse usually follows a copper-red tinged moon. They realized more children were born on full moon nights and that the moon ruled the cycles of women. They carefully registered these observations, because fertilization was vital for their survival. Some menstruation calendars originating as early as 30,000 B.C. indicate the favorable days for conception, and the number of lunar months before the predicted due date.

In the age of Cancer (circa 8,000 to 6,000 B.C.), which was ruled by the moon, home and family were important. The interrelationship between the moon and fertility was everyday knowledge. Our ancestors constructed irrigation systems for their fields using the connection between the moon's position and humidity. They domesticated chickens, goats, and pigs. They tamed cattle and started systematic breeding. They used the lunar calendar to figure out the best dates for brooding eggs and slaughtering animals.

In the fourth millennium B.C., people knew the art of grafting trees, which is a requirement for growing fruit and wine. Our ancestors who lived close to the sea understood that the tides depend on the moon. They understood that the spring tide always occurs at the full moon, and that the full moon is the ideal time for fishing. They noted all these observations in their chronicles, first on their cave walls and later (around 5,000 B.C.) imprinted in wet clay.

The rhythm of the moon, with its coming and going, gave the ancient people an idea of the great mysteries of life. The lunar phases became the symbol of the eternal cycle: procreation, birth (the small crescent on the horizon), growth (the waxing moon to the full moon), ailing and dying (the waning moon), death (the three moonless nights of the new moon), and rebirth (the reappearance of the moon after the moonless nights). Thus, the moon goddess became the ruler of the life-giving waters, the creeks as well as the oceans. She became the archetypal principle of femininity, and the most powerful figure. She was the great goddess whom most civilizations revered and worshipped under different guises for thousands of years—more than any other deity. In her bright phase, she gave life and fertility; in her dark phase, she symbolized the destructive forces of nature in the eternal cycle of death and rebirth.

How the Zodiac Was Invented

Around 4,000 B.C., it was obvious that the dates gained by observing the seasons and lunar phases were no longer sufficient. Exact timing was necessary for pioneering inventions, such as grafting plants and sowing different grain species. The astronomers of Sumeria searched for further heavenly clues in the starry sky. At first, this seemed hopeless. With a few exceptions, the stars moved year after year in the same order. They seemed to circle around the earth, but the distance between them stayed the same. The slight changes that a physical eye could detect were too minor to contribute any practical value. Nevertheless, the Sumerians registered the importance of these fixed points in the sky, and eventually developed a heavenly system in which they put single stars together into constellations. They recognized forty-eight constellations, structured by the sun's orbit and the tropics of Cancer and Capricorn. These stars served as mere reference points. The Sumerians did not discern any influence over earthly events. No one thought of observing the moon's orbit through the constellations. Instead, people made a different pioneering discovery.

For decades, scientists of the twentieth century have puzzled over the meaning of the rows of stone, several miles long, in Carnac, Brittany. There are 2,750 *menhir* (monoliths), some of which are huge, placed in a strange formation. Even more mysterious is the meaning of the stone rows and circles of Stonehenge in Salisbury. Consisting of heavy sandstone blocks, some weighing as much as five hundred tons, they were quarried in Wales, two hundred miles away, and were somehow transported to the holy site in southern England—and this in 3,000 B.C.!

Many theories have sought to explain the strange order of the mysterious stone circles and stone rows, but no explanation has been convincing. Just a few years ago, with the help of a computer, it was demonstrated that the magic holy site of Stonehenge was also a gigantic megalithic calculator. The formations of Stonehenge and other megalithic sites in western Europe were placed so that light could fall inside only during special sun or lunar positions. Astronomically trained priests were able to calculate the summer solstice and the annual movements of the planets to determine the dates for sowing, and to predict solar and lunar eclipses and other important lunar occurrences. This knowledge imbued them with tremendous power.

Not all the riddles have been solved. We still cannot comprehend how our ancestors were able to calculate with the aid of their megalithic computer. Some scientists assume that they could even have calculated the tides on the dangerous shores of England. This would have increased the success rate of fishing harvests, enabling them to break previous records. One thing is certain, however: their knowledge went far beyond our modern imagination!

The astronomers of Stonehenge and Carnac were not the only ones whose unbelievable achievements made history. At about the same time, the Babylonians built their so-called ziggurats—five to seven tiered edifices, from which their astronomers could study the sky and calculate the movements of the planets with surprising accuracy. Even the pyramids in Egypt were not just royal tombs; they were probably also astronomical observatories.

Illustration 13
A Stargazer

The Beginnings of Astrology

The zodiac came into being as a means to measure time. Nobody knows how it also became a tool to classify personalities and to interpret the future. We only know that the first personal horoscope was made in 400 B.C. This, of course, would not have been possible without the discovery of the planets.

The Planets

Early astronomers discovered the planets thousands of years ago. Those five bright stars in the night sky were unmistakable, yet they did not seem to fit into any astronomical system. They appeared to turn around the earth in the manner of the fixed stars (in reality, of course, they turned around the sun). However, their movements looked bizarre. Their orbits noodled around in the sky with regular but apparently illogical movement. From the earth, they appeared to occasionally slow down or stop suddenly, and then go backward for a while before they returned to their old courses.

Sumerian astronomers named these strange wandering stars (today we call them Mercury, Venus, Mars, Jupiter, and Saturn). They declared them to be gods and observed them carefully to find out what they signified for humanity. Thus, the planets, like the sun and moon, acquired their mythological character. Mercury was designated the fastest, smartest, and moodiest god. Mars was the master over war and violence. Jupiter was the lord of the planets. Saturn had the reputation of being cruel and irritable. When these associations became common knowledge (as, for example, in the connection between the moon and fertility), they formed the basis for astrological tradition.

In 500 B.C., either the Chaldeans or the Babylonians formalized the zodiac that we still use—with a few minor changes—today. They used the twelve main constellations through which the sun and moon regularly pass. They divided them into twelve partitions of 30 degrees each, and named them after that fixed star that was in that particular partition. Originally, the zodiac's only purpose was to measure time. At some point, our ancestors realized that when the sun, moon, or one of the five wandering planets moved through these partitions, certain phenomena occurred in clusters. This gave birth to astrology.

In the following centuries, astrologers and astronomers worked together to correlate the apparitions in the sky with events on earth. For nearly two thousand years, there was no difference between astronomy and astrology. All astronomers knew something about astrology, and visa versa. *Tetrabiblos,* the first modern astrology textbook, was written in the second century A.D. by Ptolemy, a Greek-Egyptian astronomer and mathematician. He brought the influences of the planets, the houses, and the zodiac signs into a system that remains essentially the same today. Ptolemy reputedly invented the geocentric concept of the world, which placed the earth at the center of the universe. He was the first to claim that the moon circled the earth. In this he was correct, but he also claimed that the sun and the planets circled the earth, which was wrong. However, for fifteen hundred years, nobody knew any better.

Ptolemy's theory of the world was valid until the sixteenth century, when Copernicus replaced it with his discovery that the earth circles the sun. After that, astronomy changed its viewpoint of the world and introduced the so-called heliocentric system. For astrology, however, the earth remained the symbolic reference point from which to measure the movements of the planets. Also, all the references in this book have their basis in the geocentric (astrological) view of the world, in contrast with calendars and almanacs that take into account the heliocentric (astronomical) viewpoint.

This is important because there is sometimes a discrepancy of up to four days between the geocentric and heliocentric position. Thus, the moon can simultaneously be in two different signs; for example, it can be in fertile Cancer according to the heliocentric system, while it is already in infertile Leo according to the geocentric system.

Did you know?

The Precession of the Equinox

Today, due to an astronomical phenomenon, that the experts call precession, the 30° divisions of the astrological zodiac do not correspond with the twelve astronomical constellations. Today, the astrological spring equinox lies at 0° in Aries. From the astronomical point of view, it is in Pisces. Astrology is build on a geocentric model. The constellations are now merely namesakes.

Later, the Romans practised astrology. At the time of the emperors, it was so popular that, as Juvenile wrote around A.D. 100, "There are people who do not go in public or to the baths without inquiring of the ephemeris." In the following fifteen hundred years, astrology remained on the same level. No essentially new knowledge was added. In spite of strong rejection by the churches, people considered it a serious art. Universities taught it. Royal courts throughout Europe had their astrologers. Not even the cosmological discoveries of Copernicus, Kepler, and Newton could damage astrology. Whether they thought the earth or the sun was the center point of their world, the effects of astrology on humans did not change.

In the eighteenth and nineteenth centuries, astrology fell under the influence of profiteers and charlatans. The pamphlets they circulated no longer had anything to do with true astrology. They spread evil superstitions and embarrassing half-truths and successfully destroyed the good reputation astrology had enjoyed for centuries. Only the serious astrologers of our century have succeeded in restoring the reputation of this ancient art.

The Origins of Modern Calendars

For millennia, people calculated time in years, lunar months, and days. Only two thousand years ago did they begin to count the hours as well. For a long time, they only counted the hours of daylight, and not the night hours. For thousands of years, night was synonymous with darkness, uselessness, and danger. The Talmud stated in 2,000 B.C., "Never greet a stranger at night; it could be a demon." Thus, it was logical that the first chronometer was the sundial, which only counts the cloudless hours, because it measures the length of shadow the sun casts. Details such as minutes and seconds only became important a few hundred years ago.

Solar and Lunar Years Do Not Match

As impressive as the achievements of our ancestors may have been, measuring time with the aid of the sun and moon created a problem. Solar and lunar years do not match. A lunar year is 12 times 29.5 days = 354.5 days. These are eleven days fewer than in a solar year. At first this seems to be a flaw. However, because the same season started eleven days earlier each year, an increasing discrepancy accumulated over a few years. Nobody knew what was right any more. When this became clear to our ancestors, they wondered how they could combine the solar and lunar calendars. They sought a solution everywhere. The different cultures and civilizations had very complicated systems, in which years with twelve months and thirteen months alternated.

The First Step into Modern Times—the Nile Calendar

The Egyptians invented the first precise solar calendar, based on the continual reoccurrence of the rising and falling of the Nile. At the end of June, when Sirius rose with the sun, the great floods began with regularity. They lasted until the end of October and brought silt, which made an ideal time for planting. Harvest time lasted from the end of February to the end of June. Then the rains resumed. This did not correspond with the moon, but resulted in twelve months of thirty days each. The five leftover days were stuck onto the end. This was the Nile year.

This calendar functioned so well that Julius Caesar abolished the lunar calendar that had been valid in Rome until then and introduced the Egyptian model. The only essentially novel feature was that the year began on 1 January. The Julian calendar was born, although it was not precise. The average length of a year with its 365.25 days, 11 minutes, and 12 seconds was only slightly longer than the tropical solar year, the time span between two passes of the earth through the spring equinox. The Julian calendar was valid for more than fifteen hundred years.

However, throughout the centuries, the annual eleven minute difference accumulated a remarkable discrepancy. The characteristic points of the solar year no longer corresponded to the calendar. In the sixteenth century, Pope Gregory got so exasperated that he pushed through a calendar reformation. Astronomers had been working on this for one hundred years. He decided that 4 October 1582 should be followed by 15 October. This meant that, in the following spring, the equinox, which determines the date of Easter, returned to 21 March. All the moveable Christian holidays were once again in their correct places. The valid leap day (February 28) that occurs every four years always skips the millennium year (except those that are divisible by 400).

The Gregorian calendar is very precise. There is only a one-day discrepancy with astronomical time calculations after 3,333 years. Nevertheless, there was great resistance. Workers wanted their ten days of lost pay from 4 October to 14. The Protestant countries resisted acknowledging the calendar that a Roman Catholic pope had introduced. Germany adopted the calendar in 1585 in Catholic areas, and in 1700 in Protestant areas. England adopted it in 1752, and Russia in 1918. The Islamic and Jewish countries still use the lunar calendar. The Jewish calendar, which begins each month with the new moon, is so complicated that only initiates and Rabbis can understand it.

What Does the Reformed Calendar Mean to the Old Farmers Rules?

At this point, many readers may become suspicious. When the solar and lunar years do not match each other, and also do not correspond with the Gregorian year (365 days or 366 leap year days), how can the old farming rules be correct?

This is true; they are incorrect as long as they depend on certain calendar days or holidays that depend on the calendar. However, the Moon Rules that we have collected in this book do not depend on the calendar, only on the lunar phases, or the position of the moon in the zodiac. This has not changed since the invention of the zodiac 2,500 years ago.

Did you know?

Catholic Holidays According to the Moon

The moveable ecclesiastic holidays, Good Friday, Easter, Ascension, Pentecost, and the feast of Corpus Christi, are determined by the position of the moon. Since the second century, we have celebrated Easter on the first Sunday after the first spring full moon. This means that Easter is never before 22 March and never after 25 April. The other holidays depend on when Easter arrives. Good Friday is always two days before Easter. Ascension is forty days after Easter. Pentecost is fifty days after Easter. The Feast of Corpus Christi is sixty-one days after Easter.

Table 16

Holidays that Depend on the Moon 1996-2000

Year	*Good Friday*	*Easter*	*Ascension*	*Pentecost*	*Corpus Christi*
1996	5 April	7 April	16 May	26 June	6 July
1997	28 March	30 March	8 May	19 May	29 May
1998	10 April	12 April	21 May	31 May	11 June
1999	2 April	4 April	13 May	23 May	3 June
2000	21 April	23 April	1 June	11 June	22 June
2001	13 April	15 April	25 May	4 June	14 June

Good Friday: the day of Christ's Crucifixion—two days before Easter.

Easter: the day of Christ's Resurrection—the first Sunday after the spring full moon.

Christ's Ascension: forty days after Easter.

Pentecost: the outpouring of the Holy Spirit—fifty days after Easter.

Corpus Christi: a Roman Catholic ecclesiastical holiday [the tabernacle procession through the streets]—sixty-one days after Easter.

Appendix

Table 17
Moon Calendars from 1996 to 2001

In this table the days and the times are listed in which the moon enters a certain sign of the zodiac. The time is given in Greenwich Mean Time.

1996

JANUARY 1996

Date	Time	Sign	Quarter
1	16:41:32	♉	4
3	10:42:54	♊	4
5	4:29:12	♋	1
8	10:11:49	♌	1
10	4:18:24	♍	1
13	11:42:1	♎	2
15	8: 9: 54	♏	2
17	6:22:44	♐	2
19	6:15:12	♑	2
21	6:50:31	♒	3
23	6:41:24	♓	3
25	4:45:42	♈	3
27	0:54:46	♉	4
30	7:38:25	♊	4

FEBRUARY 1996

Date	Time	Sign	Quarter
1	1:23:37	♋	4
4	7:6:37	♌	1
6	1:20:24	♍	1
9	8:41:55	♎	
11	4:37:23	♏	1
13	1:45:22	♐	2
15	0:18:34	♑	2
17	0:0:14	♒	2
20	14:33:31	♓	3
22	12:41:57	♈	3
24	9:4:10	♉	3
26	3:56:57	♊	4
29	9:47:45	♋	4

MARCH 1996

Date	Time	Sign	Quarter
2	3:35:51	♌	4
5	10:12:34	♍	1
7	5:30:35	♎	1
9	1:36:22	♏	1
12	12:21:18	♐	2
14	10:37:3	♑	2
16	9:31:40	♒	2
18	8:31:2	♓	2
20	6:49:32	♈	3
22	3:51:57	♉	3
25	11:50:1	♊	3
27	5:55:11	♋	4
30	11:39:18	♌	4

APRIL 1996

Date	Time	Sign	Quarter
1	06:03:02	♍	4
3	01:22:43	♎	4
6	11:21:44	♏	1
8	09:07:11	♐	1
10	07:23:26	♑	2
12	05:49:41	♒	2
14	04:06:09	♓	2
16	01:52:56	♈	2
19	11:57:06	♉	3
21	07:21:03	♊	3
23	01:48:07	♋	3
26	07:33:39	♌	4
28	01:37:10	♍	4

MAY 1996

Date	Time	Sign	Quarter
1	09:29:58	♎	4
3	06:28:26	♏	1
5	04:43:55	♐	1
7	03:41:42	♑	1
9	02:36:07	♒	1
11	00:52:58	♓	2
14	11:42:11	♈	2
16	07:52:04	♉	2
18	03:14:03	♊	3
21	09:54:27	♋	3
23	03:43:27	♌	3
26	09:34:51	♍	4
28	04:28:15	♎	4
30	00:50:47	♏	4

JUNE 1996

Date	Time	Sign	Quarter
2	13:35:29	♐	1
4	13:24:37	♑	1
6	13:00:58	♒	1
8	11:31:50	♓	2
10	08:41:52	♈	2
12	04:42:29	♉	2
15	12:11:39	♊	2
17	06:27:31:	♋	3
19	00:18:55	♌	3
22	05:54:36	♍	3
24	00:11:38	♎	4
27	09:01:23	♏	4
29	07:13:09	♐	4

JULY 1996

Date	Time	Sign	Quarter
1	07:04:57	♑	1
3	07:32:20	♒	1
5	07:13:17	♓	1
7	05:18:32	♈	2
9	01:45:42	♉	2
12	09:15:53	♊	2
14	03:26:04	♋	2
17	09:07:22	♌	3
19	02:50:13	♍	3
22	09:05:51	♎	3
24	04:29:10	♏	4
26	01:30:58	♐	4
28	00:26:29	♑	4
30	00:46:21	♒	1

AUGUST 1996

Date	Time	Sign	Quarter
1	01:14:55	♓	1
3	00:32:45	♈	1
6	11:07:35	♉	2
8	06:16:43	♊	2
10	00:31:15	♋	2
13	06:10:54	♌	2
16	11:54:15	♍	3
18	06:09:34	♎	3
20	01:08:51	♏	3
23	10:56:42	♐	4
25	09:27:56	♑	4
27	09:18:54	♒	4
29	09:31:13	♓	1
31	08:51:57	♈	1

SEPTEMBER 1996

Date	Time	Sign	Quarter
2	06:34:28	♉	1
4	02:33:54	♊	2
7	09:15:22	♋	2
9	03:00:41	♌	2
12	08:46:22	♍	3
14	03:09:30	♎	3
17	11:05:02	♏	3
19	07:32:47	♐	3
21	05:08:39	♑	4
23	03:50:49	♒	4
25	03:14:57	♓	4
27	02:33:47	♈	1
29	00:55:40	♉	1

OCTOBER 1996

Date	Time	Sign	Quarter
2	10:41:04	♊	1
4	05:27:42	♋	2
7	11:15:44	♌	2
9	05:05:29	♍	2
12	11:59:33	♎	3
14	07:44:31	♏	3
16	04:26:39	♐	3
18	01:57:36	♑	3
20	00:05:19	♒	4
23	12:53:04	♓	4
25	11:17:28	♈	4
27	09:02:05	♉	1
29	05:40:48	♊	1
31	01:03:53	♋	1

NOVEMBER 1996

Date	Time	Sign	Quarter
3	07:18:03	♌	2
5	01:00:53	♍	2
8	07:32:15	♎	2
10	03:16:26	♏	2
12	00:19:17	♐	3
15	12:37:16	♑	3
17	11:70:56	♒	3
19	09:22:08	♓	4
21	07:09:03	♈	4
23	04:23:01	♉	4
25	00:54:38	♊	1
28	08:59:25	♋	1
30	03:14:35	♌	1

DECEMBER 1996

Date	Time	Sign	Quarter
3	08:47:35	♍	2
5	02:51:24	♎	2
8	11:12:02	♏	2
10	08:49:11	♐	3
12	07:47:07	♑	3
14	07:11:49	♒	3
16	06:06:49	♓	3
18	04:03:22	♈	4
20	01:01:05	♉	4
23	09:58:02	♊	4
25	05:02:40	♋	1
28	11:23:17	♌	1
30	05:02:14	♍	1

1997

JANUARY 1997

Date	Time	Sign	Quarter
2	10:48:38	♎	2
4	05:51:26	♏	2
6	02:36:59	♐	2
8	01:16:56	♑	2
10	01:15:48	♒	3
12	01:20:03	♓	3
14	00:22:41	♈	3
17	11:13:16	♉	4
19	06:55:39	♊	4
21	01:48:13	♋	4
24	08:03:07	♌	1
26	01:45:06	♍	1
29	07:16:56	♎	1
31	01:39:31	♏	2

FEBRUARY 1997

Date	Time	Sign	Quarter
3	10:48:17	♐	2
5	09:14:49	♑	2
7	09:16:34	♒	3
9	09:46:33	♓	
11	09:25:34	♈	3
13	07:27:15	♉	3
15	03:48:42	♊	4
18	11:03:34	♋	4
20	05:01:17	♌	4
23	10:31:19	♍	1
25	04:17:18	♎	1
28	10:52:58	♏	1

MARCH 1997

Date	Time	Sign	Quarter
2	06:32:01	♐	2
4	03:41:40	♑	2
6	02:30:56	♒	2
8	02:33:35	♓	2
10	02:46:48	♈	3
12	02:00:21	♉	3
15	12:40:01	♊	3
17	07:47:54	♋	4
19	01:55:00	♌	4
22	07:23:23	♍	4
24	01:12:26	♎	1
27	07:56:16	♏	1
29	03:25:06	♐	1

APRIL 1997

Date	Time	Sign	Quarter
1	13:38:18	♑	2
3	11:57:06	♒	2
7	10:54:18	♈	3
9	09:57:38	♉	3
11	07:38:21	♊	3
13	03:40:12	♋	3
16	10:17:00	♌	4
18	03:55:54	♍	4
21	09:46:33	♎	4
23	04:32:58	♏	1
25	00:15:18	♐	1
28	10:29:28	♑	1
30	08:15:51	♒	2

MAY 1997

Date	Time	Sign	Quarter
2	06:38:50	♓	2
4	05:24:55	♈	2
6	04:06:46	♉	3
8	02:05:32	♊	3
11	11:37:11	♋	3
13	06:17:50	♌	3
15	00:08:08	♍	4
18	05:47:25	♎	4
20	00:25:25	♏	4
23	09:34:28	♐	1
25	07:01:29	♑	1
27	05:05:26	♒	1
29	03:21:31	♓	2
31	01:35:16	♈	2

JUNE 1997

Date	Time	Sign	Quarter
3	13:29:52	♉	2
5	10:43:55	♊	3
7	06:58:39	♋	3
9	02:03:59	♌	3
12	08:01:32	♍	3
14	01:41:33	♎	4
17	08:28:39	♏	4
19	04:39:59	♐	4
21	02:19:47	♑	1
23	00:59:58	♒	1
26	14:15:04	♓	1
28	12:28:45	♈	2
30	10:01:41	♉	2

JULY 1997

Date	Time	Sign	Quarter
2	06:52:08	♊	2
4	02:55:04:	♋	3
7	10:19:07	♌	3
9	04:16:11	♍	3
12	09:42:33	♎	4
14	03:56:07	♏	4
17	12:48:17	♐	4
19	10:51:07	♑	4
21	10:11:29	♒	1
23	09:52:18	♓	1
25	08:57:22	♈	1
27	06:57:17	♉	2
29	03:48:41	♊	2

AUGUST 1997

Date	Time	Sign	Quarter
1	12:15:36	♋	2
3	06:52:46	♌	3
5	00:51:55	♍	3
8	06:14:45	♎	3
10	00:04:58	♏	3
13	07:42:15	♐	4
15	04:49:13	♑	4
17	03:42:52	♒	4
19	03:46:39	♓	1
21	03:53:08	♈	1
23	02:59:34	♉	1
25	00:35:44	♊	2
28	09:20:24	♋	2
30	03:52:51	♌	2

SEPTEMBER 1997

Date	Time	Sign	Quarter
2	09:37:47	♍	3
4	03:11:46	♎	3
7	08:58:17	♏	3
9	03:43:42	♐	3
12	13:25:37	♑	4
14	12:00:54	♒	4
16	11:59:13	♓	1
18	12:21:58	♈	1
20	11:56:32	♉	1
22	09:54:07	♊	1
24	06:06:20	♋	2
26	00:54:28	♌	2
29	06:39:26	♍	2

OCTOBER 1997

Date	Time	Sign	Quarter
1	00:13:42	♎	3
4	06:04:04	♏	3
6	00:40:11	♐	3
9	09:19:46	♑	4
11	06:42:10	♒	4
13	05:30:26	♓	4
15	05:23:21	♈	4
17	05:25:31	♉	1
19	04:28:18	♊	1
21	01:47:21	♋	1
24	09:35:24	♌	2
26	03:27:03	♍	2
29	08:50:58	♎	2
31	02:54:44	♏	3

NOVEMBER 1997

Date	Time	Sign	Quarter
3	10:20:20	♐	3
5	06:17:05	♑	3
7	03:05:07	♒	4
9	00:50:16	♓	4
12	14:12:06	♈	4
14	13:37:12	♉	1
16	12:24:31	♊	1
18	09:45:09	♋	1
20	05:24:38	♌	1
23	11:35:23	♍	2
25	05:10:28	♎	2
28	11:24:11	♏	2
30	06:42:06	♐	3

DECEMBER 1997

Date	Time	Sign	Quarter
2	02:58:40	♑	3
4	00:01:19	♒	3
7	11:34:25	♓	4
9	09:48:38	♈	4
11	08:19:44	♉	4
13	06:42:07	♊	4
15	04:16:50	♋	1
17	00:33:16	♌	1
20	07:30:32	♍	1
22	01:11:19	♎	2
25	07:01:44	♏	2
27	02:04:16	♐	2
30	12:03:19	♑	3

1998

JANUARY 1998

Date	Time	Sign	Quarter
1	09:58:52	♒	3
3	08:19:09	♓	3
5	06:38:30	♈	4
7	04:44:10	♉	4
9	02:27:51	♊	4
12	12:51:20	♋	1
14	08:35:25	♌	1
16	03:16:45	♍	1
19	08:58:50	♎	1
21	02:42:27	♏	2
24	09:51:39	♐	2
26	0‘6:25:22	♑	2
28	04:30:07	♒	3
30	03:34:33	♓	3

FEBRUARY 1998

Date	Time	Sign	Quarter
1	02:49:13	♈	3
3	01:31:41	♉	4
6	12:53:01	♊	4
8	09:15:31	♋	4
10	004:44:28	♌	4
13	11:29:25	♍	1
15	05:16:47	♎	
18	10:48:56	♏	1
20	05:11:53	♐	2
22	00:49:44	♑	2
25	12:26:03	♒	2
27	12:00:41	♓	3

MARCH 1998

Date	Time	Sign	Quarter
1	12:04:17	♈	3
3	11:31:22	♉	3
5	09:38:45	♊	4
7	06:17:18	♋	4
9	01:40:56	♌	4
12	08:12:41	♍	4
14	01:59:24	♎	1
17	07:30:02	♏	1
19	01:33:13	♐	1
22	09:19:15	♑	2
24	06:19:43	♒	2
26	05:04:56	♓	2
28	05:11:38	♈	3
30	05:35:47	♉	3

APRIL 1998

Date	Time	Sign	Quarter
1	05:01:16	♊	3
3	02:42:29	♋	4
6	11:04:54	♌	4
8	05:16:17	♍	4
11	10:47:13	♎	4
13	04:30:07	♏	1
16	10:45:45	♐	1
18	05:46:02	♑	1
20	01:50:24	♒	2
23	13:42:46	♓	2
25	13:27:40	♈	2
27	13:48:53	♉	3
29	13:28:40	♊	3

MAY 1998

Date	Time	Sign	Quarter
1	11:26:59	♋	3
3	07:31:18	♌	4
5	02:07:16	♍	4
8	07:42:30	♎	4
10	01:24:24	♏	4
13	07:47:25	♐	1
15	02:49:40	♑	1
18	11:52:33	♒	1
20	09:13:04	♓	2
22	07:48:17	♈	2
24	07:23:25	♉	2
26	07:07:28	♊	3
28	05:52:53	♋	3
30	02:56:11	♌	3

JUNE 1998

Date	Time	Sign	Quarter
2	10:28:15	♍	4
4	04:17:49	♎	4
7	09:55:46	♏	4
9	04:20:29	♐	4
12	12:27:39	♑	1
14	08:51:11	♒	1
16	05:59:14	♓	1
18	03:53:42	♈	2
20	02:32:04	♉	2
22	01:32:51	♊	2
24	00:12:21	♋	3
27	10:56:31	♌	3
29	06:15:09	♍	3

JULY 1998

Date	Time	Sign	Quarter
1	00:27:25	♎	4
4	06:04:50	♏	4
6	00:18:35	♐	4
9	08:26:12	♑	1
11	05:09:15	♒	1
13	02:40:56	♓	1
15	00:44:14	♈	1
18	13:17:08	♉	2
20	11:34:15	♊	2
22	09:20:01:	♋	2
24	06:09:08	♌	3
26	01:47:59	♍	3
29	08:21:42	♎	3
31	02:06:20	♏	4

AUGUST 1998

Date	Time	Sign	Quarter
3	08:17:20	♐	4
5	03:36:49	♑	4
7	00:16:28	♒	4
10	12:28:22	♓	1
12	11:20:29	♈	1
14	10:05:35	♉	2
16	08:17:08	♊	2
18	05:40:43	♋	2
20	02:10:01	♌	2
23	10:10:17	♍	3
25	04:29:47	♎	3
28	10:09:26	♏	3
30	04:03:43	♐	4

SEPTEMBER 1998

Date	Time	Sign	Quarter
2	11:33:17	♑	4
4	08:21:25	♒	4
6	06:45:25	♓	1
8	06:16:41	♈	1
10	05:59:12	♉	1
12	04:56:31	♊	1
14	02:37:58	♋	2
17	11:49:12	♌	2
19	06:44:51	♍	2
21	01:01:35	♎	3
24	06:43:43	♏	3
26	00:27:30	♐	3
29	07:00:32	♑	4

OCTOBER 1998

Date	Time	Sign	Quarter
1	02:49:26	♒	4
3	00:21:50	♓	4
6	14:47:19	♈	1
7	00:01:46	♉	1
9	00:10:10	♊	1
12	12:40:36	♋	2
14	08:52:58	♌	2
16	03:49:01	♍	2
19	09:55:08	♎	2
21	03:39:01	♏	3
24	09:19:25	♐	3
26	03:31:40	♑	3
29	11:30:36	♒	4
31	08:42:50	♓	4

NOVEMBER 1998

Date	Time	Sign	Quarter
2	07:45:41	♈	4
4	08:11:09	♉	1
6	08:42:39	♊	1
8	07:56:29	♋	1
10	05:12:58	♌	1
12	00:42:58	♍	2
15	06:57:45	♎	2
17	00:39:02	♏	2
20	06:23:35	♐	3
22	00:38:03	♑	3
25	08:06:12	♒	3
27	04:19:52	♓	4
29	02:02:15	♈	4

DECEMBER 1998

Date	Time	Sign	Quarter
1	01:19:27	♉	4
3	01:35:10	♊	1
5	01:33:23	♋	1
7	00:02:40	♌	1
10	09:15:28	♍	2
12	03:38:33	♎	2
15	09:14:17	♏	2
17	03:06:41	♐	2
20	09:52:35	♑	3
22	05:10:56	♒	3
24	01:14:28	♓	3
27	12:09:29	♈	4
29	10:49:10	♉	4
31	10:14:05	♊	4

1999

JANUARY 1999

Date	Time	Sign	Quarter
2	09:32:38	♋	1
4	07:47:01	♌	1
6	04:25:34	♍	1
9	11:41:31	♎	2
11	05:31:42	♏	2
14	11:21:12	♐	2
16	05:59:33	♑	2
18	01:31:19	♒	3
21	11:27:51	♓	3
23	09:01:10	♈	3
25	07:09:17	♉	4
27	05:39:46	♊	4
29	04:10:11	♋	4
31	02:08:56	♌	1

FEBRUARY 1999

Date	Time	Sign	Quarter
3	12:07:36	♍	1
5	07:15:06	♎	1
7	01:26:36	♏	1
10	07:09:01	♐	2
12	01:27:34	♑	2
15	09:54:24	♒	2
17	07:06:01	♓	3
19	05:16:17	♈	3
21	03:53:37	♉	3
23	02:25:36	♊	4
25	00:29:44	♋	4
28	11:18:50	♌	4

MARCH 1999

Date	Time	Sign	Quarter
2	07:30:33	♍	1
4	02:49:08	♎	
7	09:18:26	♏	1
9	03:05:09	♐	1
12	09:14:29	♑	2
14	04:34:16	♒	2
16	01:26:18	♓	2
19	14:30:57	♈	3
21	14:04:34	♉	3
23	13:10:42	♊	3
25	11:12:37	♋	4
27	08:04:17	♌	4
29	03:56:56	♍	4

APRIL 1999

Date	Time	Sign	Quarter
1	11:22:35	♎	1
3	05:36:23	♏	1
6	11:18:17	♐	1
8	05:11:21	♑	1
11	12:33:28	♒	2
13	09:23:21	♓	2
15	08:05:02	♈	2
17	08:08:11	♉	3
19	08:20:13	♊	3
21	07:28:00	♋	3
23	04:58:59	♌	4
25	01:01:33	♍	4
28	08:15:33	♎	4
30	02:23:37	♏	1

MAY 1999

Date	Time	Sign	Quarter
3	08:06:29	♐	1
5	01:53:33	♑	1
8	08:27:44	♒	2
10	04:15:57	♓	2
12	01:51:00	♈	2
14	01:17:44	♉	2
16	01:50:17	♊	3
18	02:04:01	♋	3
20	00:48:10	♌	3
23	10:32:30	♍	4
25	05:21:31	♎	4
28	11:22:49	♏	4
30	05:08:07	♐	1

JUNE 1999

Date	Time	Sign	Quarter
2	10:57:32	♑	1
4	05:19:40	♒	1
6	00:31:57	♓	1
9	10:57:46	♈	2
11	10:01:47	♉	2
13	10:15:57	♊	3
15	10:27:18	♋	3
17	09:22:51	♌	3
19	06:30:02	♍	3
21	01:58:57	♎	4
24	08:18:18	♏	4
26	02:03:06	♐	4
29	07:56:37	♑	1

JULY 1999

Date	Time	Sign	Quarter
1	02:24:37	♒	1
4	10:28:12	♓	1
6	07:08:55	♈	2
8	05:07:58	♉	2
10	04:18:47	♊	2
12	04:03:11	♋	2
14	03:20:50	♌	3
16	01:20:09	♍	3
19	10:19:46	♎	3
21	04:46:14	♏	4
24	10:29:27	♐	4
26	04:27:35	♑	4
29	11:34:40	♒	1
31	07:22:16	♓	1

AUGUST 1999

Date	Time	Sign	Quarter
2	04:04:26	♈	1
4	01:39:56	♉	2
6	00:01:46	♊	2
9	13:18:49	♋	2
11	11:50:55	♌	3
13	09:25:16	♍	3
15	05:41:06	♎	3
17	00:40:48	♏	3
20	06:40:08	♐	4
22	00:30:21	♑	4
25	07:26:51	♒	4
27	03:24:12	♓	1
29	00:29:11	♈	1

SEPTEMBER 1999

Date	Time	Sign	Quarter
1	12:34:55	♉	1
3	11:00:29	♊	2
5	09:18:35	♋	2
7	07:13:55	♌	2
9	04:31:35	♍	3
11	00:56:16	♎	3
14	08:37:38	♏	3
16	02:41:22	♐	3
19	08:21:14	♑	4
21	02:46:52	♒	4
24	11:49:08	♓	4
26	09:41:43	♈	1
28	08:34:27	♉	1
30	07:37:52	♊	1

OCTOBER 1999

Date	Time	Sign	Quarter
2	06:09:36	♋	2
4	03:51:37	♌	2
6	00:44:18	♍	2
9	09:38:17	♎	2
11	04:36:40	♏	3
14	10:45:27	♐	3
16	04:24:23	♑	3
19	10:37:23	♒	4
21	06:16:18	♓	4
23	03:42:43	♈	4
25	02:50:02	♉	1
27	02:46:25	♊	1
29	02:19:55	♋	1
31	00:42:07	♌	2

NOVEMBER 1999

Date	Time	Sign	Quarter
3	10:49:25	♍	2
5	06:20:01	♎	2
7	01:08:39	♏	2
10	07:19:39	♐	3
12	00:58:54	♑	3
15	06:38:33	♒	3
17	01:24:15	♓	4
20	11:39:07	♈	4
22	10:53:52	♉	4
24	11:19:17	♊	1
26	11:33:13	♋	1
28	10:27:25	♌	1
30	07:39:59	♍	2

DECEMBER 1999

Date	Time	Sign	Quarter
2	03:25:30	♎	3
5	10:18:13	♏	3
7	04:14:07	♐	4
10	09:44:07	♑	4
12	03:29:45	♒	4
15	10:17:34	♓	4
17	06:24:33	♈	1
19	04:20:13	♉	1
21	04:00:10	♊	1
23	04:32:18	♋	2
25	04:35:48	♌	2
27	03:08:16	♍	2
30	12:38:16	♎	3

2000

JANUARY 2000

Date	Time	Sign	Quarter
1	07:17:34	♏	3
3	01:13:17	♐	3
6	06:42:42	♑	4
8	00:33:39	♒	4
11	07:16:13	♓	4
13	02:49:10	♈	4
16	13:36:02	♉	1
18	12:35:23	♊	1
20	12:31:00	♋	1
22	12:22:35	♌	2
24	11:07:16	♍	2
26	08:10:59	♎	2
28	03:36:41	♏	3
31	09:44:43	♐	3

FEBRUARY 2000

Date	Time	Sign	Quarter
2	03:22:07	♑	3
5	09:21:27	♒	4
7	04:10:39	♓	4
10	13:00:48	♈	4
12	10:03:20	♉	1
14	08:01:42	♊	1
16	06:47:57	♋	1
18	05:57:44	♌	1
20	04:49:15	♍	2
22	02:37:43	♎	2
25	11:33:53	♏	2
27	05:55:10	♐	3

MARCH 2000

Date	Time	Sign	Quarter
1	11:27:14	♑	3
3	05:26:09	♒	
5	00:15:50	♓	3
8	09:32:30	♈	4
10	06:53:50	♉	4
12	04:49:12	♊	4
14	03:01:56	♋	1
16	01:20:42	♌	1
19	13:27:23	♍	1
21	10:41:25	♎	2
23	06:47:15	♏	2
25	01:40:06	♐	2
28	07:27:34	♑	3
30	01:12:48	♒	3

APRIL 2000

Date	Time	Sign	Quarter
2	08:23:39	♓	3
4	04:52:10	♈	4
6	02:39:31	♉	4
8	01:12:46	♊	4
11	14:01:54	♋	1
13	12:01:42	♌	1
15	09:28:46	♍	1
17	06:18:43	♎	1
19	02:21:17	♏	2
22	09:40:00	♐	2
24	03:33:34	♑	2
27	09:06:00	♒	3
29	03:35:40	♓	3

MAY 2000

Date	Time	Sign	Quarter
2	13:05:02	♈	3
4	11:27:37	♉	4
6	10:49:50	♊	4
8	10:12:24	♋	4
10	08:49:26	♌	1
12	06:24:42	♍	1
14	03:01:46	♎	1
17	11:23:18	♏	1
19	06:00:35	♐	2
22	11:49:11	♑	2
24	05:25:08	♒	2
27	11:47:36	♓	3
29	07:38:45	♈	3
31	05:18:21	♉	3

JUNE 2000

Date	Time	Sign	Quarter
2	04:36:53	♊	4
4	04:42:27	♋	4
6	04:25:10	♌	4
8	2:55:49	♍	4
10	00:00:47	♎	1
13	08:22:38	♏	1
15	02:52:32	♐	1
18	08:39:15	♑	2
20	02:14:47	♒	2
23	08:10:46	♓	2
25	03:14:46	♈	3
28	13:46:48	♉	3
30	12:56:20	♊	3

JULY 2000

Date	Time	Sign	Quarter
2	13:11:28	♋	4
4	13:19:32	♌	4
6	12:17:33	♍	4
8	09:36:17	♎	1
10	5:21:24	♏	1
13	11:57:47	♐	1
15	05:40:46	♑	1
18	11:09:03	♒	2
20	05:11:12	♓	2
23	12:39:42	♈	2
25	09:08:13	♉	3
27	07:07:40	♊	3
29	06:31:47	♋	3
31	06:40:19	♌	4

AUGUST 2000

Date	Time	Sign	Quarter
2	06:27:30	♍	4
4	04:53:54	♎	4
6	01:34:44	♏	4
9	08:49:05	♐	1
11	02:35:34	♑	1
14	08:04:13	♒	1
16	02:11:33	♓	2
19	09:41:16	♈	2
21	05:47:07	♉	2
23	02:55:49	♊	3
25	01:12:14	♋	3
27	00:26:33	♌	3
29	00:02:59	♍	4

SEPTEMBER 2000

Date	Time	Sign	Quarter
1	13:06:23	♎	4
3	09:53:09	♏	4
5	05:03:38	♐	1
8	10:56:19	♑	1
10	04:34:52	♒	1
13	11:02:20	♓	2
15	06:26:04	♈	2
17	02:43:43	♉	2
20	13:34:16	♊	2
22	11:35:55	♋	3
24	10:10:07	♌	3
26	08:58:41	♍	3
28	07:24:18	♎	4
30	04:44:34	♏	4

OCTOBER 2000

Date	Time	Sign	Quarter
2	00:36:45	♐	4
5	07:05:13	♑	1
7	00:42:42	♒	1
10	06:52:19	♓	1
12	02:14:23	♈	1
15	12:28:50	♉	2
17	10:18:34	♊	2
19	08:26:40	♋	2
21	06:37:56	♌	3
23	04:44:54	♍	3
25	02:35:27	♎	3
28	13:00:18	♏	4
30	08:33:21	♐	4

NOVEMBER 2000

Date	Time	Sign	Quarter
1	02:59:30	♑	4
4	08:30:52	♒	1
6	02:25:09	♓	1
9	10:16:49	♈	1
11	07:22:04	♉	2
13	05:42:19	♊	2
15	04:36:50	♋	2
17	03:23:04	♌	2
19	01:35:43	♍	3
22	12:35:00	♎	3
24	08:56:20	♏	3
26	04:25:16	♐	4
29	11:01:36	♑	4

DECEMBER 2000

Date	Time	Sign	Quarter
1	04:41:28	♒	4
4	10:19:26	♓	1
6	05:07:28	♈	1
8	01:26:45	♉	1
11	14:04:09	♊	2
13	13:47:31	♋	2
15	13:24:48	♌	2
17	12:07:02	♍	2
19	09:34:02	♎	3
21	05:48:43	♏	3
23	01:03:35	♐	3
26	07:32:42	♑	4
28	01:16:01	♒	4
31	06:42:33	♓	4

2001

JANUARY 2001

Date	Time	Sign	Quarter
2	00:53:50	♈	1
5	09:26:33	♉	1
7	07:16:43	♊	1
9	06:46:24	♋	2
11	07:07:44	♌	2
13	07:07:35	♍	2
15	05:46:00	♎	2
17	02:41:56	♏	3
20	10:26:01	♐	3
22	04:29:22	♑	3
25	09:57:26	♒	4
27	03:38:09	♓	4
30	09:55:11	♈	4

FEBRUARY 2001

Date	Time	Sign	Quarter
1	05:09:23	♉	1
3	01:44:25	♊	1
6	14:43:18	♋	1
8	15:00:01	♌	2
9	00:15:04	♍	2
11	00:07:59	♎	
14	11:45:53	♏	2
16	07:14:56	♐	3
18	01:29:37	♑	3
21	06:54:52	♒	3
23	00:36:49	♓	4
26	06:59:58	♈	4
28	02:03:36	♉	4

MARCH 2001

Date	Time	Sign	Quarter
3	11:23:16	♊	1
5	09:10:09	♋	1
7	08:18:30	♌	1
9	08:18:46	♍	2
11	08:05:34	♎	2
13	06:30:47	♏	2
15	03:03:37	♐	2
18	09:58:42	♑	3
20	03:37:15	♒	3
23	09:15:41	♓	3
25	03:45:01	♈	4
28	11:55:12	♉	4
30	08:18:42	♊	4

APRIL 2001

Date	Time	Sign	Quarter
1	05:30:30	♋	1
3	03:36:52	♌	1
5	02:33:44	♍	1
7	01:50:44	♎	1
9	00:33:50	♏	2
12	10:57:21	♐	2
14	05:56:16	♑	2
17	11:43:12	♒	3
19	05:28:06	♓	3
22	12:22:17	♈	3
24	08:12:29	♉	4
26	04:57:39	♊	4
28	02:23:57	♋	4
30	00:20:03	♌	1

MAY 2001

Date	Time	Sign	Quarter
3	12:53:14	♍	1
5	11:18:25	♎	1
7	09:10:41	♏	2
9	05:58:18	♐	2
11	01:27:46	♑	2
14	07:45:39	♒	2
16	01:27:59	♓	3
19	07:54:39	♈	3
21	03:32:32	♉	3
23	00:26:56	♊	4
26	12:36:20	♋	4
28	11:11:47	♌	4
30	09:39:49	♍	1

JUNE 2001

Date	Time	Sign	Quarter
1	07:42:41	♎	1
3	05:06:22	♏	1
5	01:38:24	♐	1
8	09:35:50	♑	2
10	03:49:14	♒	2
13	09:26:32	♓	2
15	03:31:27	♈	3
18	11:36:19	♉	3
20	08:50:03	♊	3
22	07:26:12	♋	4
24	06:47:43	♌	4
26	06:04:00	♍	4
28	04:33:47	♎	1
30	01:57:51	♏	1

JULY 2001

Date	Time	Sign	Quarter
3	11:02:27	♐	1
5	05:57:59	♑	2
7	00:12:56	♒	2
10	05:52:15	♓	2
13	11:47:58	♈	3
15	06:45:25	♉	3
17	03:08:21	♊	3
19	01:13:56	♋	3
21	00:47:40	♌	4
23	00:56:35	♍	4
25	00:30:53	♎	4
28	12:10:52	♏	1
30	08:05:24	♐	1

AUGUST 2001

Date	Time	Sign	Quarter
1	02:54:46	♑	1
4	08:59:05	♒	2
6	02:42:19	♓	2
9	08:27:10	♈	2
11	02:53:34	♉	2
14	11:38:55	♊	3
16	09:32:24	♋	3
18	09:07:20	♌	3
20	09:37:07	♍	4
22	09:41:18	♎	4
24	08:12:44	♏	4
26	04:51:45	♐	1
29	12:08:17	♑	1
31	06:02:01	♒	1

SEPTEMBER 2001

Date	Time	Sign	Quarter
3	11:35:49	♓	2
5	05:31:00	♈	2
8	12:13:49	♉	2
10	07:42:15	♊	3
12	04:28:12	♋	3
14	02:51:51	♌	3
16	02:43:59	♍	3
18	03:08:36	♎	4
20	02:43:31	♏	4
22	00:31:37	♐	4
25	08:50:26	♑	1
27	02:55:43	♒	1
30	08:28:45	♓	1

OCTOBER 2001

Date	Time	Sign	Quarter
2	02:26:38	♈	2
5	09:19:22	♉	2
7	04:41:52	♊	2
9	00:55:30	♋	2
12	12:27:57	♌	3
14	11:42:13	♍	3
16	11:31:28	♎	4
18	10:48:42	♏	4
20	08:36:42	♐	4
22	04:38:53	♑	4
25	11:14:47	♒	1
27	04:57:56	♓	1
30	11:00:35	♈	1

NOVEMBER 2001

Date	Time	Sign	Quarter
1	05:51:45	♉	2
3	01:30:10	♊	2
6	11:23:18	♋	2
8	08:56:00	♌	3
10	07:14:34	♍	3
12	06:05:38	♎	3
14	04:54:45	♏	3
16	02:56:26	♐	4
19	12:26:16	♑	4
21	07:07:47	♒	4
23	01:02:41	♓	1
26	06:51:02	♈	1
28	01:30:39	♉	1

DECEMBER 2001

Date	Time	Sign	Quarter
1	10:28:57	♊	2
3	07:44:30	♋	2
5	05:42:16	♌	2
7	04:01:18	♍	3
9	02:22:44	♎	3
11	00:28:55	♏	3
14	11:28:10	♐	4
16	07:36:54	♑	4
18	02:42:22	♒	4
21	08:50:15	♓	4
23	02:35:52	♈	1
26	09:15:02	♉	1
28	05:09:05	♊	1
30	02:31:04	♋	2

Bibliography

American/British Sources

Boorstin, Daniel; *The Discoverers* (Vintage, 1985)
Campbell, Joseph; *The Masks of God, Occidental Mythology* (Penguin, 1976)
Collins, Laura; *Herbs* (Aura, 1992)
Christmas in Today's Germany (World Book, Inc., 1993)
Cunningham, Donna; *Moon Signs* (Knaur, 1992)
Cunningham, Scott; *Llewellyn's Magical Almanac 1993* (Llewellyn, 1985)
Cunningham, Scott; *Cunningham's Encyclopedia of Magical Herbs* (Llewellyn, 1994)
Fell, Derek; *The Encyclopedia of Flowers* (JG Press, 1995)
Fenton, Sasha; *Moon Signs* (Aquarian, 1988)
Frazer, J.G.; *The Golden Bough. The Classic Study in Magic and Religion* (Papermack, 1990)
Geddes, Sheila; *Astrology and Health* (Foulsham, 1992)
George, Demetra; *Mysteries of the Dark Moon* (Harper, 1992)
Golowin; *The World of the Tarot: Secret Teachings of the 78 Cards of the Gypsies* (Weiser, 1982)
Goodman, Linda; *Linda Goodman's Star Signs* (St. Martin's Press, 1987)
Greene, Liz; *The Astrology of Fate* (Weiser, 1983)
Greene, Liz; *Astrology for Lovers* (Mandala, 1991)
Guiley, Rosemary Ellen; *The Lunar Almanac* (Piatkus, 1991)
Katzeff, Paul; *Moon Madness* (Citadel, 1981)
Lieber, Arnold; *The Lunar Effect* (Anchor, 1978)
Leek, Sybil; *The Complete Art of Witchcraft* (Goldmann, 1985)

Llewellyn's 1996 Organic Gardening Almanac: Gardening by the Moon (Llewellyn, 1995)
Llewellyn's 1997 Moon Sign Book (Llewellyn, 1996)
Llewellyn's 1997 Magical Almanac (Llewellyn, 1996)
Llewellyn's 1997 Daily Planetary Guide (Llewellyn, 1996)
Lust, John; *The Herb Book* (Bantam Books, 1974)
Markale, Jean; *Merlin, Priest of Nature* (Inner Tradition, 1989)
Marron, Kevin; *Witches, Pagans and Magic in the New Age* (Seal, 1990)
Michel, Peter, Ph.D.; Ecclesiastic reference
Michelsen, Neil F.; *The American Ephemeris for the 20th Century* (ACS, 1988)
Michelsen, Neil F.; *The American Ephemeris for the 20th Century* (ACS, 1994)
Michelsen, Neil F.; *The American Ephemeris for the 21st Century* (ACS, 1992)
Parker, Julia & Derek; *New Complete Astrologer* (Random House, 1990)
Parker, Julia & Derek; *Parker's Astrology* (Dorling Kindersley, 1986)
Parker, Julia & Derek; *The Power of Magic: Ancient Secrets and Modern Mysteries* (S&S Trade, 1993)
Webster's New International Dictionary of the English Language, 2nd Ed. Unabridged (G & C Merriam Co., 1946)
Webster's New World Dictionary, 2nd. College Ed. (Simon & Schuster, 1986)
New Saint Joseph Sunday Missal (Catholic Book Publishing Co., 1995)
Parker, Julia & Derek; *Parker's Astrology* (Dorling Kindersley, 1991)
Riotte, Louise; *Astrological Gardening* (Storey, 1989)
Talbot, Michael; *The Holographic Universe* (Harper Collins, 1992)

German Sources

Appel, Walter A.; *Im Zeichen des Mondes* (Goldmann, 1985)
Appel, Walter A.; *Die Macht des Mondes* (Goldmann, 1989)
Bauer/Dümotz/Golowin; *Lexikon der Symbole* (Heyne, 1987)

Benjamin, Alexander; *Das große Buch vom Vollmond* (Knaur, 1990)
Braungger, Günther; *Lehrbuch der Astromedizin* (München, 1984)
Gabriel, Ingrid; *Kosmische Einflüsse auf unsere Gartenpflanzen* (Falken, 1986)
Hämmering, Elisabeth; *Mondgöttin Inanna* (Kreuz, 1990)
Hendel/Foss-Hendel; *Astro-Diagnose* (Darmstadt, 1978)
Klein, Nicholas/Dahlke, Rüdiger; *Das senkrechte Weltbild* (Hugendubel, 1986)
Kreuter, Marie-Luise; *Wunderkräfte der Natur* (Heyne, 1977)
Paungger, J./Poppe, T.; *Vom richtigen Zeitpunkt* (Hugendubel, 1991)
Roscher, Michael; *Der Mond* (Hugendubel, 1988)
Schiffmann, Philip; *Mondkalender für das Jahr 1993* (Wien, 1992)
Schiran; *Menschenfrauen fliegen wieder* (Knaur, 1988)
Sharamon/Baginski; *Kosmobiologische Geburtenkontrolle* (Windpferd, 1991)
Sulzberger, Robert; *Kosmos Gartenkalender 1993* (Franckh, 1992)
Thun, Maria; *Aussaattage 1988* (Biedenkopf, 1987)
Valentinitsch, Helfried; *Hexen und Zauberer* (Leykam, 1987)
Wendel, Mathias/York, Ute; *Maskenball der Seele* (Knaur, 1993)
Wohlgenannt, Hermann; *Der Mond und seine Bedeutung in der Astronomie und im Volksglauben* (Teutsch, 1990)
York, Ute; *Dünger und Kompost* (Pawlak, 1992)
York, Ute; *Kräuter* (Pawlak, 1992)

Italian Sources

Baccelli, Sesto Cajo; *Il vero Sesto Cajo Baccelli, Guida dell'Agricoltore. Lunario per l'anno 1993* (Ofiria, 1992)
Barbanera; *L'Astronomo di Foligno 1993* (Campi, 1992)
Paltrinieri, Mario; *Oroscopo 1993 del Sole e della Luna* (Pratica, 1992)
Vincenzi, G.; *Nuovo Calendario Lunare delle Semine e delle lavore* (Casa Verde, 1992)

Index

R

S

T

U

V

W

Y

Z

Moon Phases

Symbol	*Terminology*	*Terminology in This Book*
○	new moon	first quarter
◐	waxing half moon	second quarter
●	full moon	third quarter
◑	waning half moon	fourth quarter

Signs of the Zodiac

Symbol	**Name**
♈	*Aries*
♉	*Taurus*
♊	*Gemini*
♋	*Cancer*
♌	*Leo*
♍	*Virgo*
♎	*Libra*
♏	*Scorpios*
♐	*Sagittarius*
♑	*Capricorn*
♒	*Aquarius*
♓	*Pisces*